NUFFIELD
ECON
& BUSI

CW01095321

Business Strategies

How are decisions made?

LONGMAN

Copyright acknowledgements

The Nuffield Economics and Business Project team and the Publishers are grateful to the following for permission to reproduce copyright material:

FT Business Enterprises Ltd for extracts from articles in the *Financial Times* 3.8.93 and 26.4.94; Ford Motor Company for an extract from *Statement of Vision and Values*; Guardian Newspapers Ltd for extracts from the articles 'Hidden memory in store' by Nicholas Bannester in the *Guardian* 1.5.93 and by Stephen Halliday in the *Guardian* 18.4.93; Newspaper Publishing plc for adapted extracts from articles 'Scenarios make the future feel familiar' by Paul Miller in *Independent on Sunday* 24.3.91, 'Ethical money urged to target offending firms' in *Independent on Sunday* 17.1.93; Penguin Books Ltd and the author's agents for an extract from *Managing on the Edge* by Richard Tanner Pascale (Viking 1990), © Richard Pascale, 1990.

Acknowledgement is also due to the *Independent on Sunday* for Figure 4.14 and to the following for permission to reproduce illustrations on the pages indicated:

Business Humour and John Morris for pp. 9 and 98; WH Smith for p. 12; Financial Times for p. 54; Geoff Ward for p. 97.

Cover photograph: Paul Brierley

Addison Wesley Longman Limited
Edinburgh Gate,
Harlow, Essex, CM20 2JE, England
and Associated Companies throughout
the world.

© The Nuffield Foundation 1995

ISBN 0 582 24583 4

First published 1995
Second impression 1996

Designed and typeset by
Ken Vail Graphic Design, Cambridge

Printed in Singapore by Longman
Singapore Publishers Pte Ltd

The Publisher's policy is to use paper
manufactured from sustainable forests.

Contents

Acknowledgments

This book was written by Alison Wood with a substantial contribution from David Lines.

We would like to thank all the people who helped and advised during the writing of this book. Special thanks are due to Peter Hall of Peter Hall Strategic Management, who introduced us to the science and art of decision making.

We are grateful to everyone in the Economics and Business Studies Department at Queen Mary's College, Basingstoke.

A number of people read and commented on early versions of the book and their help was invaluable. In particular, David Myddleton, Ian Chambers and Stephen Barnes made many useful contributions and we are most grateful for their help. Jill Turner also helped greatly in many ways.

The help and support of our administrator, Linda Westgarth, whose contributions were so many and so great that they cannot be briefly described, were essential to both the development work and the final preparation of the book for publication.

Nancy Wall
Editor

About this book

The resources which have been developed by the Nuffield Economics and Business Project are designed specifically to support the Nuffield A levels in Economics and Business. These courses are examined by London Examinations. Although written for a particular course, the book may be found useful by anyone who is studying A level Business Studies, or who is interested in the subject matter.

This book is one of a series of six designed to support the course options. It covers Option 5, and if studied with Option 6, *Corporate Responsibility: Is business accountable?*, leads to an A level in Business Studies. It can also be combined with any of the four other options, so leading to a joint A level in Economics and Business.

The book is intended to underpin about ten weeks' work in the later stages of the A level course. It assumes that the reader has a working knowledge of the fundamentals of business. An understanding of the phases of the business cycle will also be helpful. The book can be read in conjunction with any introductory business text but fits neatly alongside the *Student's Book* written for the Nuffield Project.

Nuffield Economics and Business courses require students to investigate themes and issues in order to achieve an understanding of the subject matter. So the book is structured around five Enquiries.

Enquiry guide

Each of the five enquiries in this book is intended to take on average two weeks of subject time. The precise nature of the Enquiry is to be determined by you, the reader. You will need to consult a variety of sources: other books, databases, newspapers and periodicals. If you have access to IT databases and to CD-ROM you will find these helpful.

The questions

Each Enquiry opens with questions, presented in diagrammatic form so that the links between them are made as clear as possible.

These questions highlight important issues and perspectives which can be investigated during the Enquiry. They are not exhaustive in scope, and they tend to be rather general. You will need to break them down into subsidiary questions, which you should arrange in a logical order. You can create a hierarchy of questions and then ask yourself:

- how are these questions related to each other?
- which are the most important?
- can they be answered with the information available?
- what other information will be needed in order to illuminate the issues?

Opening evidence

The opening evidence presents a range of quotations, public statements, data and case studies. Different points of view are laid out and the data cover a number of the angles which will need to be considered. Again, the opening evidence is not exhaustive: the reader who pursues the Enquiry diligently will find much other relevant information elsewhere.

You can use the opening evidence to help you get started on your investigation, and to get a feel for the issues which are a part of your Enquiry. It should raise the questions in your mind which will become the main focus of your Enquiry.

The text

The text forms the main body of this book and underpins the Enquiry. It does not, for the most part, provide answers to the questions. But it does present a good deal of information which can be *used* to answer the questions. You must take this information, together with your prior knowledge of the subject, and the fruits of your enquiries, and build them into an evaluation of the issues.

In the early part of the Nuffield course, the way in which decisions were to be tackled has often not been an issue. It was assumed that people would approach decision taking in an appropriate way. Here the emphasis changes. You are encouraged to look for the most constructive approach for the situation in hand, keeping in mind the overall context of the business. It should not be assumed that profit maximisation is always the primary aim. There may be other important considerations.

In the margins, beside the text, you will find references to various concepts. This is an indicator that you will need to use these ideas in order to understand fully the events described.

Also in the margins you will find 'Open Questions'. These are questions which do not have a simple answer but which should be considered carefully. They relate to issues upon which agreement cannot necessarily be expected, but which it is important to discuss.

The outcome

The important thing to remember is that you must think everything through for yourself. In this book, we have looked at the work of management 'gurus' – people who write about business and put forward new ideas about how businesses should be organised. Do try to read at least some of their work. Tom Peters has a very easy style and, as well as being useful for your business studies, is a thumping good read. John Harvey-Jones, of *Troubleshooter* fame, tells an excellent story. If you find a particularly good bit, make a note of the reference – it can be kept in a card index – so that, when you are writing an essay, you can find relevant information easily.

Ideas about business date rather quickly. One of your major tasks is to find out how thinking has changed since this book was written. New issues will have come to the forefront of consciousness in the business world, and new solutions will have emerged. Don't ever accept anything that you read unquestioningly. No one in business ever has 'the answer'. The latest 'wonder theory' soon turns into 'yesterday's news'. If you read business studies books from a few years ago, you will often find that companies which are highly praised are the ones facing real problems today. Read Peters, read Porter, read Harvey-Jones – read whatever you like – but always *think about it for yourself!*

Suggested reading

There are many good business books, but the following will start you off in the right direction:

Tom Peters, *Thriving on Chaos,* Pan Books, 1987
Richard Pascale, *Managing on the Edge*, Penguin, 1990
Richard Pascale and Anthony Athos, *The Art of Japanese Management,*
    Business Library, 1991
M. E. Porter, *Competitive Advantage*, Macmillan, 1985
John Harvey-Jones, *Making It Happen*, Collins, 1988
T. J. Peters and R. H. Waterman, *In Search of Excellence,*
    Harper & Row, 1982
John Harvey-Jones, *Managing to Survive*, Heinemann, 1993
T. E. Deal and A. A. Kennedy, *Corporate Cultures – The Rites and*
    Rituals of Corporate Life, Penguin, 1988

Ideally, you should find that your enquiries do not stop when you have finished this book, but become a basis for further thought and for a continuing watch on business decision making in the future.

Enquiry 1: How does decision making begin?

Scope

It is easy to believe that all successful businesses are the result of inspired judgement or innate skills on the part of the entrepreneur. Some are, of course, but making good and effective decisions is a skill, and one that can be learned. This Enquiry will lay the foundation for acquiring that skill. The initial task is to ensure that the problem itself is not too big, and therefore soluble. For that, information has first to be acquired, and then processed by breaking it down into manageable proportions. Modern technological aids can help in this but an understanding of the way data can be analysed manually is also important.

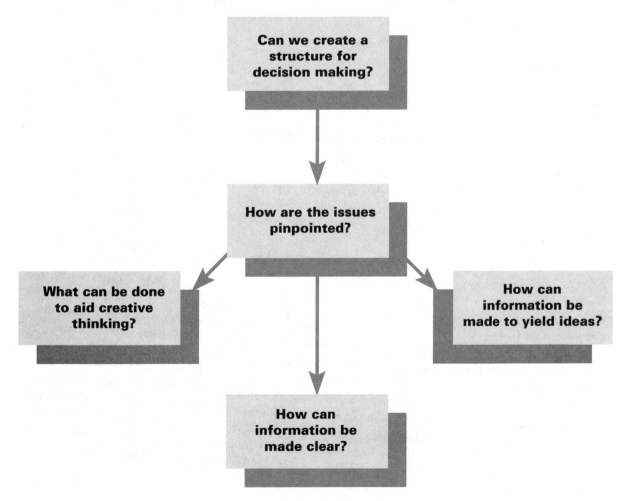

Opening evidence

> *Question:*
> How do you eat an elephant?
> *Answer:*
> One bit at a time.

> 'Sometimes the problem is so huge that you don't know where to start. You just sit and worry and don't do anything at all and *that's* the real problem.'

FPI Painters and Decorators

FPI is a firm of painters and decorators. Potential customers ring up and ask for estimates for work. The owner of the business, Ian Price, then visits the customer, looks at the job and produces an estimate which includes labour and materials. This is sent to the customer, who has probably asked several firms for quotations.

Customers do not necessarily choose the cheapest estimate. They look at the range of prices quoted and choose the one which represents the best value for money.

FPI has found recently that fewer and fewer of its estimates are being accepted. Ian has telephoned potential customers to find out why. They have told him that FPI's prices are much higher than other firms.

As Ian puts it, 'The *problem* is: our estimates are too high. Customers are going elsewhere. The *question* is: how can we lower our costs?'

> 'An organisation is a collection of choices looking for problems, issues and feelings looking for decision situations in which they might be aired, solutions looking for issues to which they might be the answers, and decision-makers looking for work.'
>
> Source: James G. March, quoted in D. S. Pugh and D. J. Hickson, *Writers on Organisations*, Penguin, 4th edition, 1989

The Recycled Bike Company

Jamie Bolan had always loved bikes. He spent his childhood doing them up for his friends and when he left school he set up the Essential Bicycle Co. He knew the bike world well - holidays were spent working in a bicycle shop and he had always read all the cycling magazines.

There seemed to be seven distinctive kinds of 'bike people'. There were children, who were buying bikes for themselves, and parents buying for children. There were 16–25 year olds – often students. There were adults – some bought bikes for fun and others for travelling to work. There were 'serious cyclists', who went to specialist shops and spent hundreds of pounds. And there were 'Greens' – people who used bikes because they were ecologically sound.

There were seven categories of bike, too. Bikes for little children – tricycles and scooters – and bikes for older children. There were 'working' bikes, with baskets and racks. There were 'fun' racing bikes, which cost a few hundred pounds and 'fun' mountain bikes for the same price. Then there were professional racing and mountain bikes, at high prices.

'Problems are only opportunities in work clothes.' – Henry J. Kaiser, 1882–1967

'The last meeting I went to was about falling sales. I thought that we were there to do something about it. Oh no. We spent the whole morning arguing about what exactly the problem was. It was the sales manager who started it. We'd just got our coffee and sat down, when he began yelling at the production manager – going on and on about the quality of the new machines. The production manager said that it wasn't the quality of the production, but the design of the machines which was wrong, which set the designer off. He said that there was no point in designing a new machine if sales didn't bother to come in and learn about it. The trouble was that sales didn't understand the new equipment, so weren't pushing it hard enough to the customers. It just went round and round in circles. The meeting broke up, with nothing agreed. If we can't even agree what we are going to talk about, I don't see how we can agree about anything else.' – Robert McEvoy, Customer Services Manager of a large computer company

'I am the MD of a medium sized company, so I make decisions every day. We make high fashion clothes, so I have to survive in a rapidly changing market. I rely on my managers to provide me with information and recommendations and so my decision is only as good as that input. Fashions change all the time, so I have to make decisions and commit resources now and keep my fingers crossed that I am right about the future. My biggest problem is that it takes time for information that I need to be gathered. We have to balance getting that information quickly with getting that information right.'

TINA (There Is No Alternative) situations have no place in a book about decision-making and decision-makers. If there truly is no alternative, no decision needs to be taken. For decisions are choices. The act of decision presupposes that alternatives exist.

Source: Robert Heller, *The Decision Makers*, Coronet, 1989

In reality, creativity and innovation are as teachable as accountancy, and far more rewarding in terms of profitable corporate growth. Simon Majaro, the author of *The Creative Gap*, offers two basic definitions: that creativity is the thinking process that helps to generate ideas; and that innovation is their practical application in order to meet the organisation's objectives more effectively. The important word in the first definition is 'process'. It's possible to organise the search for innovation as thoroughly as any hunt for acquisitional targets.

Source: Robert Heller, *The Decision Makers*, Coronet, 1989

1 Analysing the problem to gain an advantage

Everyone makes decisions every day. As with many 'everyday' activities, people tend to take decision making for granted and seldom examine how they make decisions. Everyone is so busy thinking about the content of their decisions – what their decision making is about – that they do not pay any attention to the process – the steps they go through to arrive at their decision.

If you want to improve your decision making, you can spend time looking at the content, or at the process. Time spent looking at the content will help you to improve a particular decision, but time spent looking at the process will help with every decision. This is because the content is specific to each decision, whilst the process can apply to any decision. If a business wants to improve its decision making capability, it must undertake this process more effectively. This book will examine the ways in which businesses make decisions and will consider how they might improve their decision making.

Issue diagrams

Sometimes a problem seems so huge that there is simply no obvious place to begin to tackle it. The only way is to divide the main issue up into smaller units – sub-issues. If those sub-issues are too large to tackle, they can be divided into further sub-issues. This process carries on until, instead of one huge problem, there are a whole range of small problems. Each small problem is definite and manageable. This is then called an **issue diagram**.

Fixed and variable costs

FPI Painters and Decorators

Ian Price, of FPI Painters and Decorators, uses an *issue diagram* to set out his problem and to break it down into manageable parts. He begins with the main issue – how can FPI reduce their costs? He then splits this down into smaller questions, such as, what are the fixed and variable costs? Those are split down into even more specific questions. The further across the diagram he moves, the more the questions are solution-oriented. He ends up with some very specific ones. They are manageable. He can look at the costs and benefits of employing two secretaries, in comparison with employing one more productively. He can find out the buying and running costs of diesel vans, instead of petrol ones. In Figure 1.1 each 'arm' contains more detail until a manageable question is reached. This diagram illustrates the principle. In practice each question could generate many further ones.

Figure 1.1 FPI's issue diagram

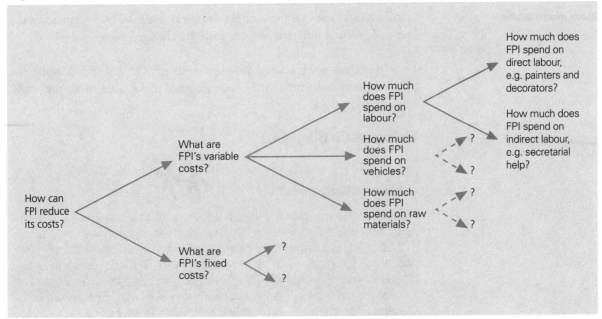

Issue diagrams can be used to address many different kinds of problems. Some, such as: 'How can the profitability of our products be increased?' are so broad that a series of issue diagrams will be needed. The first is a *profit diagram*, as shown in Figure 1.2, setting out the different ways of increasing profitability.

Figure 1.2 A profit diagram

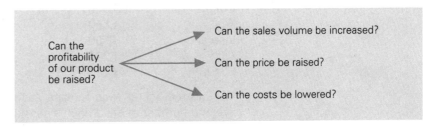

The sub–issues are then taken and split into lower level questions, which can be investigated individually. Perhaps some are not a problem – the workforce may be very well trained and working efficiently. If so, this can be eliminated from the discussion. The real problem may be that the machinery is inadequately maintained, or out of date.

The issue diagram enables an investigation of the problem to be carried out in the most appropriate way. For instance, the question of training can be addressed by looking at the way the staff work and asking them how confident they feel about their skills and whether they would like more training. A price elasticity question can be investigated by looking

Elasticity

Break even analysis

at past information about the effects of price changes, or at price elasticity figures from similar industries. The effect on sales of raising prices can be calculated and the company might use break even analysis to indicate the levels of profit at different outputs with the changed prices.

• Issue diagrams split a large problem into smaller ones, but once the problem is manageable, it is essential to make sure that the right questions are asked.

Using issue diagrams

Sheila McCarthy's school

Sheila McCarthy owns a nursery school in the suburbs of a large city. She has a two-session day: the morning session is from 9.00 to 12.00 and the afternoon session is from 1.00 to 4.00. At full capacity, she can take 80 children, from 3 to 5 years, in each session and she charges £5.00 per session. Children can come for as many sessions per week as they like and Sheila provides facilities for them to eat a packed lunch if they stay all day.

The school is open from Monday to Friday during school terms – 195 days a year. Sheila works all day, every day and is helped by eight full time staff (paid £12,000 a year each).

Sheila's costs per month are:

Mortgage	£600
Wages (staff)	£8,000
Fuel	£150
Insurance	£100
Toys	£200
Food	£200

In 1986 the school was running at full capacity but since then the average number of children in a session has fallen:

Year	1986	1987	1988	1989	1990	1991	1992
Average number of children per session	80	78	75	70	70	60	55

Sheila has no idea why this situation has developed or what she can do about it.

Draw an issue diagram to help Sheila to set out her problems more clearly.

Using the issue diagram, suggest to her what information she needs to gather before beginning to make any decisions.

Asking the right questions

There was certainly a problem in Robert McEvoy's meeting (see Opening evidence). Everyone accepted that there was a problem, but no one agreed on what that problem was. Kenichi Ohmae, in *The Mind of the Strategist,* says that if you want to find the solution to a problem you have to ask the right questions. The trouble in business is that people seldom ask the right question.

He gives an example: the amount and cost of overtime working has been rising and a company needs to make decisions about how to reduce it. A question is framed: 'How can we reduce overtime working?' Some people suggest that employees should be made to work harder during normal hours, or that the lunch time should be shortened or that private telephone calls should be banned.

Ohmae argues that the proposed 'solutions' are not very helpful. They deal with 'symptoms'. A 'symptom' is a small issue, which is not the real problem. Vague and unspecific questions lead to an unproductive discussion about symptoms, with each person going on and on about an issue which concerns him or her but which, in the general scheme of things, is fairly unimportant. Objectively, people are seldom that lazy at work so shortening lunch time will make little difference and, over a whole day, a few personal phone calls are not that important.

Ohmae suggests that a question like 'Is the company's workforce large enough to do all the work required?' is far more helpful. It is specific and makes clear the kind of information that is needed to answer it. It is a 'solution based question'. The information to answer it would concern levels of production, hours worked and the number of employees. This information could be obtained by looking at comparable businesses.

Thinking creatively

Breaking down the problem into manageable parts and asking the right questions allows space for creativity and originality because it separates 'the wood from the trees'. Jamie Bolan of the Recycled Bike Company did just this, having researched his market to find out about his potential market and customers.

The Recycled Bike Company

Jamie drew a product-market matrix, as shown in Figure 1.3, showing the customers, and which markets they were in.

Figure 1.3 A product-market matrix

Products / Consumers	Children under 8 years	Children 9–16 years	Working bikes	Fun racing bikes	Professional racing bikes	Fun mountain bikes	Professional mountain bikes
Children – buying for themselves		✓		✓		✓	
Parents – buying for children	✓	✓		✓		✓	
16–25 years old			✓			✓	
Adults 25–65 – leisure use						✓	
Greens			✓			✓	
Adults – travel to work			✓	✓		✓	
Serious cyclists					✓		✓

'Fun' mountain bikes looked a good option, because the market for them was large. The problem was that you could buy 'fun' mountain bikes in most cycle shops, probably for less than Jamie could sell them – it was the same with 'fun' racing bikes. Children's bikes were too small a market and he would be competing with toy shops. He didn't have the expertise or the capital to supply professional mountain or racing bikes.

That left 'working bikes'. Jamie looked at the matrix. Working bikes were used by adults travelling to work and by Greens. Then Jamie had an idea.

He had always thought that people wanted to buy new, flashy bikes, with the most up to date equipment and smart paint finishes. It now occurred to him that this might not be so. Greens might like second hand bikes, because they were recycled. People using bikes to travel to work really did not want conspicuously

expensive bikes, because they would be stolen from the cycle racks. What were needed were reliable, safe, ordinary bikes, at low cost, that could be repaired easily.

If he could find a supply of second hand bikes, he could do them up and then sell them on. He could provide a repair service and market them as 'Green' bikes.

He spent a few days going around the local area, checking the competition and couldn't find any. Quite a few of the cycle shops were selling second hand bikes – as 'part exchanges' on new bikes – but they looked in very poor condition. He chatted with some of the owners, who expressed an interest in selling the bikes to him cheaply, just to get them off their hands.

In 1989, he leased a shop and set up business. He now owns three shops and is planning to buy a fourth.

Jamie's decision making was creative. It was not based on looking at cost and revenue projections, or on finding some new ways to compete with existing businesses. The product–market matrix provided a way to help him to think creatively.

'Better put out notepads and pens in case any of them has an idea.'

Source: John Morris, *Funny Business*, Business Humour, 1992

He looked at the market for bikes in a completely new way, casting aside previous ideas about what was 'obvious'. In the past everyone had assumed that people wanted new bikes, or the very cheapest second hand bikes. It occurred to Jamie that they only bought new bikes because second hand ones had such a poor reputation. Give them second hand bikes with a guarantee of quality and they would buy.

Jamie's decision was based on looking at the market with new eyes and making an imaginative leap from the matrix which he had in front of him. Rather than getting it to tell him what to do, he used a decision making technique to help himself to think creatively.

Keeping ahead of your competitors

When managers break a problem down into smaller parts and think creatively, they will do so in competition with other businesses. Some businesses have found that the technique actually helps them to compete more effectively in their market and to keep ahead of their competitors.

Keeping ahead of the rest

Tony Banbury works for one of the largest manufacturers of television sets. He is a development engineer and his job is to think of more and more ways of improving televisions.

'Look at your TV set. What could you do to make it better? Basically, you've got three choices. You can improve the quality of the picture – flat screens, all that kind of stuff. You can improve the sound – better reproduction, or just make it louder. You can change the packaging – it used to be teak boxes, now it's matt grey.'

Tony's company uses the idea of **strategic degrees of freedom** to help it decide how to improve its products.

'Picture, sound and package are the three ways of improving TVs. We use a diagram, showing these three strategic axes. Each axis is called a strategic axis of freedom and we put the various possible improvements on to each axis.' (See Figure 1.4 on page 10.)

Figure 1.4 Strategic axes of freedom

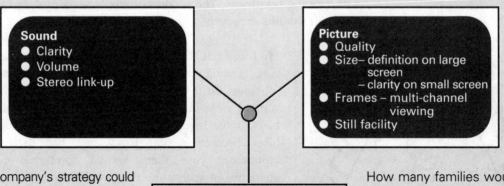

Sound
- Clarity
- Volume
- Stereo link-up

Picture
- Quality
- Size– definition on large screen
  – clarity on small screen
- Frames – multi-channel viewing
- Still facility

Packaging
- Range of colours
- Co-ordinated
- Non-scratch plastic
- Effect on sound quality

'Our company's strategy could be to improve or develop any aspect of our televisions. We use the diagram to set out the different areas where we could develop our products to gain strategic advantage over our competitors.'

His company is competing with other manufacturers, in a market where technology is changing fast. Companies are innovating and so no one is sure which way the market will move. Tony's company has to make decisions about which aspect of the televisions it will concentrate on. Resources are limited and it needs to make sure that any improvements will increase profitability.

'There are all sorts of improvements which we could make, from really ordinary things, like on-screen boxes so that you can watch more than one channel at a time, to televisions which can act as 'videophones' – you and your granny in Australia can chat to each other through the television.'

The technology is there to develop such new ideas, but a company does not want to waste time and money developing new products, simply to find that there is no market for them.

How many families would be prepared to pay for a television that would let them talk to granny, when they can telephone her for a few pounds?

There is no point in a company working on improving areas where another company has far more advanced technology.

'We look at what our competitors are doing in each area. Who is emphasising what in their advertising? Who is ahead of us and who is behind us in each area. We reckon that, as long as we're at least keeping up with whatever everyone else is doing on each of our strategic axes, we're safe.'

Of course, a business cannot know what its competitors have got planned for the future.

'We do try to predict what's going to happen in the market. You try to forecast what your competitors are going to do. If we think someone is going to launch something new, we have to decide if we want to try to pre-empt them, or get something better onto the market, or move into a different market ourselves and avoid competition.'

The SAF diagram does not tell a business which strategy to pursue – this is a matter for imaginative and incisive thinking. It acts as a tool, to set out the possibilities for the management team.

Using SAF diagrams

The Non-stop Grocery Store

The manager of the college shop is talking to one of her colleagues about Non-stop, a 24-hour grocery store that has opened up next door to the college.

'The problem with Non-stop is that they can sell a far wider range of confectionery than we could hope to stock. Their stationery is cheaper, even though they do not have the range that we have. They are selling sandwiches and cakes at lunchtime, which are good, even though they are expensive. I am really worried that students will choose to shop there, instead of coming to us.'

Draw an SAF diagram for the college shop. Besides the issues covered in this conversation, what other areas of competition might there be?

In which areas might the college shop be able to compete effectively and how?

What do you think the strategic axes of freedom for the following products might be: a) sound systems; b) ready-prepared meals; c) personal stereos?

Open Question

What is it about creative thinking that leads to higher profits?

2 Gathering information

Questionnaires

Market research

If you ask most people how businesses gather information, they will tell you about market research – making up a questionnaire and selecting a sample of people to ask. Clearly market research is a vital business activity. The problem is that carrying out a survey is only one way of gathering information and, some people argue, not the most effective or efficient way.

Market orientation

The aim of market research is to find out as much about the market as possible. This enables a firm to be *market led* – to tailor its product to the wants and needs of the customers. If you know what your customers want, you can ask yourself 'Is what I am doing giving my customers what they want?' You use the wants of your customers as a criterion for decision making.

Using information technology

One of the easiest ways of finding out what customers want is to look at what they are actually buying. We have looked at how SAFs can help companies to gain competitive advantages over others; now we shall look at how companies use information technology to speed up and improve their decision making processes.

Hidden memory in store

'THANK you, Sir. I'll have the watches wrapped. I trust you found the pink shirts pleasing?' A sales assistant in a Dunhill shop completes a sale for a well-heeled customer.

But that check on a previous purchase? Brilliant memory on the part of the salesman ... or just good technology?

For when the sub-total is totted up on the discreetly hidden electronic till, the assistant is automatically reminded of a customer's previous purchase.

Dunhill knows the value of the personal touch. Traditionally, its staff recorded their customers' preferences and purchases in a private notebook. But when staff left, the information went with them.

Leading retailers at an ICL conference earlier this week were intrigued by a glimpse of the mysterious world of Dunhill.

Dunhill is soon to introduce barcodes on its goods after a long debate about whether they detract from the characteristic atmosphere of a Dunhill shop. However the barcode readers are likely to be out of sight, joining the EPOS tills behind traditional wooden fittings.

While Dunhill has harnessed technology to improve its personal service, WH Smith has developed a computer system called Bookfinder, which could lead to customers ordering and paying for books, cassettes and CDs without any help from sales staff.

Bookfinder is to be installed in Smith's stores from July onwards. Initially, it will be used by staff to check whether a book is in stock or has to be ordered. The order is initiated by a keystroke. No longer will copious paperwork be needed.

Smith's says Bookfinder, which cost in excess of £1 million to develop, could easily be used by customers direct. However, this service is unlikely to be introduced until it has a proven bug-free track record, and methods to check customers' credentials have been agreed with banks.

The key problem for Smith's was establishing an up-to-date database. They have merged two well known book lists with their own database. The group is seeking to extend the system to cover

recorded music, but faces a huge task in creating a full database, since the music publishing business is notoriously fragmented.

Retailers have a touching belief that customers enjoy 'the shopping experience' and that technology can enhance it – even if it involves enquiring about pink shirts.

Source: Adapted from Nicholas Bannister, in the *Guardian*, 1 May 1993

In what ways do EPOS (Electronic Point of Sale) systems help:
a) low volume, high price businesses;
b) high volume, low price businesses with their decision making?

Businesses try to gain competitive advantage over others in the market and information technology can help, both by speeding up the decision making process and by making more and better information available.

Sharing information

It is usually assumed that every company has its own information, which it uses itself and guards jealously from its competitors. If information is power, organisations will want to keep their information to themselves.

Not all businesses have found this to be so. Some find that sharing information with other businesses can be beneficial to everyone.

Sharing information

Most supermarkets now have scanners at the tills, linked to computers. The till operators pass goods over these scanners, which read the bar codes. The bar code tells the computer what goods have been purchased and the computer supplies the price.

This computerised system can be used for stock control. As an item is purchased and comes off the shelves, a new item can be ordered from the supplier automatically.

One large supermarket chain, like many other businesses, finds this information invaluable. It has also found that it is not always beneficial to keep the information it gathers to itself. It shares information with other businesses and the combined data have been used to build a model for forecasting demand for products.

The combined information from a group of businesses is far more powerful than individually gathered data. Competitive advantage does not lie in information itself, but in the use a company makes of that information.

Product life cycles

It is not only information about what customers are buying that is important. Traditional market research, which tells you what your customers have done in the past, is becoming inappropriate. In some markets, product life cycles are shrinking and the market is changing so rapidly that there simply is no time to find out what people want, design a product, test it, research people's perceptions of it and then launch it.

To be successful, a business needs to be in such close contact with its market that it knows what is happening in that market and what customers want without having to go out and carry out research.

IBM

IBM has been a highly successful and profitable company, but in 1992 it announced its first-ever operating loss and measures were put into place to deal with the problems.

While computers were expensive mainframes IBM was the clear market leader. Profit margins were excellent and, given the high costs of entry into the market, there was little new competition. The company was product led, with customers buying what IBM was able to produce.

With the demise of the mainframe and rise of the personal computer, IBM's fortunes changed. Competitors could produce PCs more cheaply than IBM and these companies were market led – producing what the consumer wanted to buy.

Instead of products being developed and launched over a period of 18–24 months, timescales in the computer market have been slashed to 6 months

There is little time for IBM to develop new products itself in top secret laboratories and then launch them on the market. Instead, IBM invites its customers to presentations, where they learn about new product developments.

IBM finds out from its customers what they want and, in conjunction with them, develops those products – it has become consumer *responsive*. Instead of the customers only meeting sales people, they talk to staff from the development laboratories. The people who will be buying IBM products talk directly to the people who are developing them.

Interviewed for television, Dave Schleicher, Director of Development at IBM, in Rochester, Minnesota, USA, said: 'We were making some decisions about product direction and we found that we were guessing. We divulge company secrets in these meetings, we ask for advice, we ask for criticism. We get a lot of both – in some cases, more of the latter than the former! But it is constructive. It allows us to go back and change our plans and strategies.'

IBM has a 90-day Callback system, whereby people who have bought equipment are telephoned 90 days after receiving the goods and their opinions are sought. It was through this Callback system that IBM learnt that its customers wanted to be able to attach non-IBM printers to IBM mini-computers, and so could begin research work on how this might be done.

IBM also works with its competitors. The Somerset project involved an alliance between IBM and Motorola, working on a new family of microprocessors. In a television interview, Bob Mansfield, the Project Manager, said: 'Long gone are the days when you could count IBM's competitors on one hand and it was pretty easy to say, "Well amongst those five people, I know pretty much what's going on."'

It simply is not possible to know what is going on in such a rapidly changing market by 'doing market research'. The only way to keep ahead of the technology is to work with people who are on the leading edge of that technology. IBM learns about the market from its competitors and collaborates with those competitors, to their mutual advantage.

Gossip

Information is power. If a business knows what its competitors are going to do, it can outmanoeuvre them; if it knows what will happen in the future, it can position itself to benefit. Good information is vital for decision making.

But information is problematic – it is expensive and time consuming to gather – but, more importantly, people have a very narrow view about how to find things out.

Hot gossip

How important is 'gossip'? One executive puts it this way:

'If I want to know what is happening where I work, I can read the weekly bulletin. I can check all the notice boards. I can write memos to the management, asking specific questions and hope that they will reply. But, if I really want to know what is happening, I tap into the gossip!

'Gossip' has got a bad name. Most people think it means 'silly chit-chat'. In fact, tapping into the proper 'gossip' will give you all kinds of information which is not available through the official channels.

'All this talk about business executives "networking" amuses me. When I started work, I "networked" with other women in the company. We swapped ideas and information and helped each other out. There weren't many of us, compared with the men, and we felt left out, so we banded together. The men would say, "Look, the women are gossiping again." Women gossip; men network!

'There is gossip in business. Who is doing

what ... who is working where ... who is thinking of moving ... who is discontented ... who is being secretive and why ... what do people think is going to happen?

'To make it seem more business-like, we'll agree to call it "networking". You don't just network within your company. It is equally important to network within your market and within the business community as a whole. Not all information will be useful; not all information will be correct, but the more you are exposed to what is happening, the more you will be able to decide what is good and what is bad information.

'So, what should you do? First, keep a close watch on the technical literature in the field. Go to conferences and seminars. Don't just listen to the speakers; talk to the other delegates. Watch what your competitors are doing. Get hold of their brochures and keep an eye on their advertising. Watch what the leaders in the field are doing. Don't forget to monitor the smaller, leading-edge companies. Listen to what your people tell you. What are your customers telling your sales people? What are the people who are not your customers saying?'

3 Processing information

Of course, it is not enough just to gather information. Sometimes it is possible to have too much to process effectively and indeed in some organisations the target becomes the acquisition of data as an end in itself.

Using information effectively

The case study which follows demonstrates both the strengths and the weaknesses of gathering information to aid decision making.

Newtown College

Imogen Penfold is the Principal of Newtown College. Over the past few years, the College has come under increasing pressure to generate income by selling its education and training services to industry. Imogen explains the situation thus:

Market research

'Three years ago, we commissioned some market research, to find out what training needs there were in our area. These needs turned out to be IT, modern languages and leisure courses for the growing number of unemployed. Of course, we jumped straight on to the IT bandwagon – we had the expertise, we could easily acquire the hardware and it looked like a way of printing money. The report was filed away.

'We invested in a new IT suite and did some advertising. It did work, to a degree. The problem was that other businesses in the area had got the same results from their market research and were doing exactly the same as us. We could only compete with the big computer companies on price and, frankly, that wasn't the customers' main concern. We hadn't a chance in a highly competitive and rather over-crowded market.

'With hindsight, we should have gone for the modern languages. We had the information – it was in black and white in the report. But we jumped on the most obvious need shown by the research. If we'd gone for modern languages, we wouldn't have been in competition with anyone.'

Newtown College made a decision, on the basis of carefully (and expensively) collected information, but they did at least two things wrong. First, they did not do any competitor analysis – they assumed that, if there was a need in the market, they would be the only ones to fill it. They never thought that other people would have done the same market research and come to the same conclusions.

Second, they had a structural problem. David Ho, the Head of Modern Languages explains:

'Companies in Newtown are doing more and more business with Europe and business language courses are few and far between. For years, I had been saying, "There's a market out there for modern language courses." The problem was that I didn't have a forum in which to say it.

'I didn't even know we'd done any market research. If I'd known we were looking for new openings, I would have said, "Let's go for modern languages." Instead, senior management paid for a report, took a look at it and, of course, their first thought was, "Oh, look, IT – we can do that". It's too late now – the money was spent on computers. If we'd invested in a language lab, we'd have no competition and could expand in that market.'

David had foreseen a need for modern language classes, but Newtown College had no way of gathering information from its own staff. Instead, it spent money on expensive market researchers. Had there been some mechanism for disseminating information from the report through the staff, David would have come forward.

Instead, senior management kept information to themselves. This was not a deliberate attempt to hide anything from the staff – it was because it did not occur to management that there was anything to be gained by giving staff access to this information. Imogen again:

'The lesson we learnt was that, to be useful, information must be *fluid* and *run freely* through the organisation. Instead of being static – a report in a filing cabinet in my office – it must be dynamic. I should have sent copies of the report to the Heads of Department. They should have returned it, with comments. I should have collated the comments and put a discussion document together. We should have

Communication

called a meeting and let everyone see what could be done. Really, we should have let the report become a resource for the College – a springboard for creative thinking by everyone. The report should have been less important than the dialogue between management and staff stimulated by it. We'll know better next time!'

In the same way that a country's infrastructure – its roads and railways – enables people and goods to move from place to place, an information infrastructure enables information to permeate the whole organisation.

So this is what Newtown College created. Imogen describes the changes:

'We had to set up new teams – one to deal with services to industry, another to look at ways of getting Newtown College involved with community projects. All sorts of different areas were covered by these new teams. Some people accused us of simply making more meetings.

Teamwork

'But these teams were different. They were *ad hoc*. Each team would have a core of members, but the other members were either invited along because they had specialist knowledge or skills, or invited themselves along because they had an idea they wanted to try out. Instead of groups being from within departments in the College, they were from across departments. For the first time, we had people from science working with people from languages, or business education or whatever.'

These teams were *interdisciplinary* and *task oriented*. Instead of looking at what would be most beneficial for their departments, team members would be concentrating on the task in hand – how to benefit the College as a whole.

John Walker, Management Information Systems Manager, explains the situation:

'These new structures had enormous information implications. We set them tasks – or they set themselves tasks – and we have to give them the information to make decisions. Previously confidential information – perhaps on the College's funding or on costs – had to become open information. The teams couldn't make decisions if they had no idea about the constraints.

'The IT network was probably the most important tool for these teams. Storing the information centrally, but enabling people to use it across the College meant that everyone had access to exactly the same information. It could be updated easily and once the central data were updated, we were sure that everyone else's data were current.'

It is not just financial information which is stored centrally. Minutes of meetings, notices about future meetings and information gathered by different groups is also stored centrally – to be accessed by everyone. Anyone can see what other groups are doing and, if they feel it would be helpful, can become involved.

Decentralisation

Because information is freely available across the College, Newtown has been able to allow decisions to be made institution-wide. Each team has access to the data needed to make decisions and is responsible for inputting more about what it is doing, so that everyone is aware of what is happening. The College believes that it has gained competitive advantage through its IT systems. It is a large institution which thinks and acts like a number of small ones.

Imogen Penfold again:

Open Question

How might IT lead to poorer rather than better decision making?

'Our most recent success was when a large Japanese company moved to the area. One of our staff heard about this and fed the information to our Industry Links group. They put together a "Japanese Culture" day-school to inform firms about Japanese business practices and customs.'

Dealing with large quantities of data

The Newtown College example showed that acquiring data did not in itself lead to better decision making. It is often the presentation of data that is in itself confusing. Take the following example. Two businesses have the sales shown in Figure 1.5.

Figure 1.5 Sales

Business A		Business B	
Week	**Units sold**	**Week**	**Units sold**
1	16	1	16
2	14	2	16
3	9	3	14
4	16	4	13
5	14	5	12
6	5	6	16
7	28	7	14
8	28	8	16
9	16	9	16
10	16	10	17
11	14	11	14
12	12	12	14
13	9	13	12
14	6	14	13

The figures for Business A could be described by listing the sales for each week, but that would be time consuming. It would be easier to find some way of 'summing up' the data in a more concise way.

One way of doing this is to talk about the average sales figure. This can be done by calculating the **mean** or arithmetic average which, for Business A, is 14.5. (Add the units sold and then divide the total by the number of weeks.)

But, if you calculate the mean for Business B, it is 14.5 too.

Both Business A and Business B can be described as having an average sales figure of 14.5 units a week, but their actual sales look very different. The mean is a useful way of describing data, but two sets of data can have the same mean, yet be very different. This could lead to very real business problems. For instance, if managers were using the mean number of units sold per week as the basis for ordering, they would run into problems of over- and under-ordering on a week-to-week basis.

There are other ways of talking about a set of data. One method is to talk about the **mode** – the value which appears the most often. It might be a useful way of describing the number of units sold in the example of the two businesses. Unfortunately, for Business A, the mode is 16. But it is 16 for Business B also.

Another way is to talk about the **median**, which is the value which splits the data into two equal halves. To work out the median, arrange the data in order and then select the middle value. But the median for Business A is the same as that for Business B – 14 units.

The mean, median and mode seem incapable of giving a description that is simple and concise, yet which retains a complete picture of the actual data. This is because these averages only tell us where the *centre* of the data lies. We would also need to know the highest and lowest values and the range (the distance between them). For Business A, the lowest weekly sales were 5, the highest 28 and the range (28 − 5) = 23. For Business B the lowest is 12, the highest 17, the range only 5.

It is often useful to know the consistency of the data too: in other words, the amount by which the values collectively deviate from the mean. The range goes part of the way in telling us this: Business B's weekly sales are indeed at a more consistent level than Business A's. However, the range only takes account of two values (the highest and lowest), and these may be extreme. The statistical method of measuring the degree of deviation of the data as a whole from the mean is known as the **standard deviation**.

Suppose for instance that there are two groups of students, and the mean height of each group is the same – 1.63m. This information *could* conceal the fact that the students of one group were all within say 5 cm above or below 1.63m, while the students in the other were all within

±15 cm of 1.63 m. Unless the heights of the tallest and shortest students were *very* untypical of the values as a whole, the heights of the students in the first group, taken collectively, would show a smaller deviation from 1.63 m than those in the second group. The standard deviation of the first group would be less than the standard deviation of the second. Another way of expressing this would be to say that if the standard deviation of the first group is 1 cm, and of the second is 5 cm, then a student chosen at random from the first group is just as likely to be 1 cm above the mean as a student chosen from the other group is to be 5 cm above the mean. Figure 1.6 shows this.

Figure 1.6 Measuring dispersion

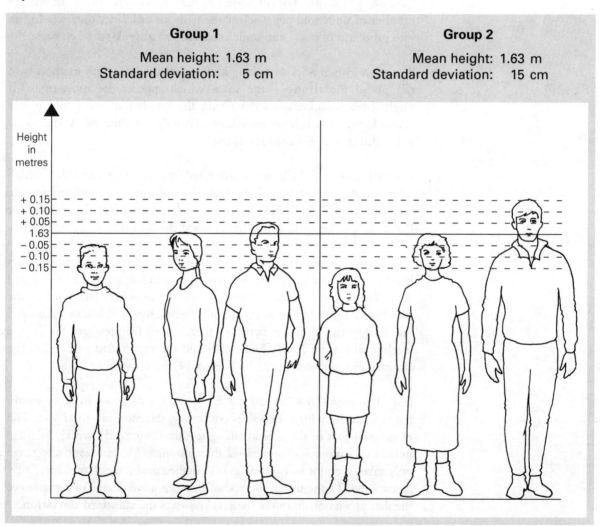

Group 1
Mean height: 1.63 m
Standard deviation: 5 cm

Group 2
Mean height: 1.63 m
Standard deviation: 15 cm

Height
in
metres

+ 0.15
+ 0.10
+ 0.05
1.63
− 0.05
− 0.10
− 0.15

The standard deviation is calculated in the following way:

1 First, calculate the mean. For Business A, it is 14.5.

2 Then calculate how much each value in the data differs from the mean – see Figure 1.7. For example, the value for week 1 is 16 units. This is 1.5 units greater than the mean.

Figure 1.7 Deviation

Week	Units sold	Deviation from mean
1	16	1.5
2	14	−0.5
3	9	−5.5
4	16	1.5
5	14	−0.5
6	5	−9.5
7	28	13.5
8	28	13.5
9	16	1.5
10	16	1.5
11	14	−0.5
12	12	−2.5
13	9	−5.5
14	6	−8.5

3 The obvious way to calculate the standard deviation would be to add up all the individual deviations and then divide this by 14. The problem is that, if they are added up the answer always comes to 0 (try it, if you don't believe it). So, to get rid of the + and − signs, square the deviations (multiply them by themselves) – see Figure 1.8.

Figure 1.8 Standard deviation

Week	Units sold	Deviation	Squared deviation
1	16	1.5	2.25
2	14	−0.5	0.25
3	9	−5.5	30.25
4	16	1.5	2.25
5	14	−0.5	0.25
6	5	−9.5	90.25
7	28	13.5	182.25
8	28	13.5	182.25
9	16	1.5	2.25
10	16	1.5	2.25
11	14	−0.5	0.25
12	12	−2.5	6.25
13	9	−5.5	30.25
14	6	−8.5	72.25

4 Add up these squared deviations.
For Business A, this comes to 603.5.

5 Divide this by the number of values:

$$\frac{603.5}{14} = 43.11$$

6 Then calculate the square root of this number:

$$\sqrt{43.11} = 6.57$$

The mean number of units which Business A sells each week is 14.5, with a standard deviation of 6.57 units.

Business B has a mean of 14.5, with a standard deviation of 1.59.

The mean and standard deviation are together a useful way of describing a set of data. They tell you what the average is and how much the data, as a whole, differs from that average.

Knowing the mean and the standard deviation is useful, but it is tedious to work out. The way around this is to buy or borrow a calculator which automatically calculates the standard deviation of any data which you enter into it. However, an understanding of the theory which lies behind the calculation is absolutely essential.

4 Extracting the information from the data

Talking about data in terms of mean, median, mode and standard deviation is a useful way of referring to and coping with a great deal of information in a concise way.

Sometimes it is not the quantity of data which is problematic. It is the fact that the information contained in the data is obscured by the data itself; and information for decision making is no use if it is unclear or difficult to understand.

Figure 1.9 shows the sales figures for a business. Sales are rising, but the magnitude of the figures makes it difficult to see by how much they are rising, year on year. The way the data is presented makes the information which is being conveyed almost impossible to see.

Index numbers   Converting the data into **index numbers** makes the information clearer. Index numbers take one item of data (usually the first item in a series) and use this as the base, which is given the number 100. In this example the base period is 1980.

Subsequent items of data are related to the base period. The sales figure for 1980 is 11,876, which is given the index number 100. The figure for 1981 is 12,978, which can be converted into an index number using the formula:

$$\frac{\text{Value for the year you are interested in}}{\text{Value for the base period}} \times 100$$

For 1981, this will be: $\dfrac{12,978}{11,876} \times 100 = 109$

Really, all this is doing is calculating percentage increases. If 11,876 is 100%, then 12,978 must be 109%.

The other index numbers can be calculated on a spreadsheet making the information far easier to interpret. For instance, sales have grown from 100 to 291 in 12 years, as shown in Figure 1.9. That is an increase of 191%.

Figure 1.9 Sales and indices

Year	Sales	Index
1980	11,876	100
1981	12,978	109
1982	13,224	111
1983	14,794	125
1984	14,667	124
1985	15,765	133
1986	18,321	154
1987	18,555	156
1988	19,509	164
1989	21,558	182
1990	22,549	190
1991	25,581	215
1992	34,599	291

With index numbers it is possible to make comparisons between like and unlike quantities. Suppose that the managing director felt that the reason why these sales figures have risen so dramatically is because the sales team had eaten more and more chocolate.

She has collected data on chocolate consumption and so the easiest thing to do would be to plot the sales figures on a graph and plot chocolate consumption on the same graph to see whether there is any link.

The problem is that she cannot plot unlike quantities on a graph. One axis would show time and the other could not show both sales figures and quantity of chocolate eaten. It could, however, show an index.

Figure 1.10 Index numbers for chocolate consumption

Year	Chocolate bars	Index
1980	250	100
1981	190	76
1982	256	102
1983	180	72
1984	120	48
1985	200	80
1986	93	37
1987	180	72
1988	229	92
1989	165	66
1990	88	35
1991	186	74
1992	99	40

Using the spreadsheet, the index numbers for chocolate consumption have been calculated, as shown in Figure 1.10.

Figure 1.11 shows sales figures and chocolate consumption. Clearly, and unsurprisingly, there is absolutely no correlation (i.e. direct relationship) between the figures.

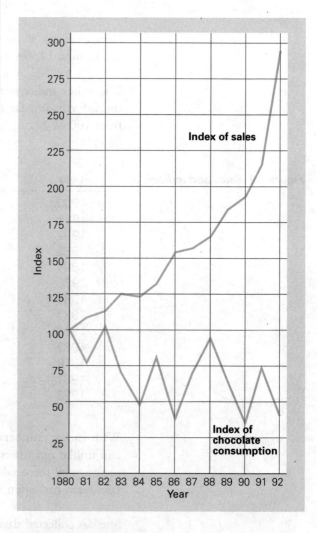

Figure 1.11 Sales figures and chocolate consumption

How technology improves information quality

We have looked at the problems which businesses have when faced with volumes of information and we have looked at ways of processing that information to reduce the quantity to a manageable level. The problem with doing this is that the processing can obscure very important detail in the information.

The information revolution and electronic shopping

IN the US, you can do your shopping without leaving home. You simply pick up your telephone and tell Tootsie what you want. She takes your order, agrees a method of payment and then tells the warehouse to send whatever you want.

The Home Shopping Network (HSN) is the main player in the $1.3 billion electronic shopping business. HSN promotes its products on television and Tootsie is the electronic voice that shoppers hear when they ring up to order goods. If shoppers are unwilling to talk to a computer, they can speak to a human operator instead.

There are obvious advantages. HSN does not have to build and maintain huge supermarkets for its customers to browse in and customers should receive a fast, efficient service. There

is an additional benefit. Each detail of every transaction is processed by the computer, so can be easily electronically logged. The management of HSN have a huge bank of data which is up-to-the-minute and available immediately. This can be used as the basis for decision making in the business.

HSN's data is updated every ten seconds. The hosts of the TV 'infomercials' can see how well the products they are promoting are selling. If sales are slow, the hosts can switch to another line or change their sales pitch. Sales progress can be monitored in terms of 'dollars per minute' of TV time.

In the UK, McDonald's, the fast food chain, is using IT to improve the flow of information between its

restaurants and head office; point of sales (POS) equipment has been upgraded to enable this to happen.

McDonald's used to rely on performance indicators, based on averages from each store. Management made decisions on the basis of the average number of customers in a store, the average number of people who were satisfied or dissatisfied, the average amount of waste. Averages were used because it was simply far too difficult to gather and process detailed information. The problem was that the use of averages masked either very good or very poor service during the course of the day. New IT systems enable McDonald's to gather and process the vast amounts of information that are necessary, if averages are not used.

Source: *Financial Times*, 3 August 1993

Why is HSN's system of home shopping beneficial for both the customer and for HSN itself?

How has the use of IT improved both the service which customers receive in McDonald's and the efficiency of the business itself?

Why has using 'real' data instead of averages improved the quality of McDonald's decision making?

Using a decision making model

Gardener's question time

'We're in real trouble,' said Geoff, the production manager of Garden Tools Ltd. Everyone else agreed. 'I mean,' he continued, 'look at our product range? Sales for the sit-on mower are pretty stagnant – we were the leader in the field once, but the market's saturated now. It's making us money, but I'm not sure how much longer it can go on.'

'Yes,' agreed Mike, his assistant, 'but at least we're making money. The petrol-driven mower's actually losing us money.'

'We really need to move into a new area,' said Kate, the trainee manager. 'We are doing quite well with the heavy duty strimmers. Sales have been rising steadily and our model is lighter and easier to use than anything else on the market. Can't we build on that?'

'That's a good idea. I've been thinking about how we could apply "strimmer" technology to hedge cutting – if only we could make them small enough to lift easily, but powerful enough to cut through twigs. The trouble is that we are simply not generating enough profit to invest in research and development.'

'We need to think about this systematically,' said Kate. 'We've been doing this on my course.' She got out her folder. 'Here, it's in with marketing. We need to set out the problem and then look at the 4 Ps.'

Using any model that you think appropriate and helpful (and not only the kinds of models which you have looked at in this chapter!), set out the problem clearly. How can Garden Tools Ltd go about solving its problem?

4 Ps

Boston matrix

This Enquiry has looked at how businesses might structure their decision making, so that the process is more effective. It is now necessary to look at the kind of information which they will need to gather before they can make their decisions, and the methods they might use to do so.

Enquiry 2: What is to be decided?

Scope

All too often decision making in firms is a response to a situation – sales and profits are falling, or a competitor has entered the market with a new product – rather than being part of a plan for the future. This kind of crisis management can result in an organisation lacking any sense of direction. It is therefore vital for firms to look ahead so that their decisions can be based around a proactive rather than a reactive stance. This Enquiry looks not only at how firms must organise themselves in order to have clear and achievable aims and objectives, but also at how they must co-ordinate their actions, so that they all pull in the same direction.

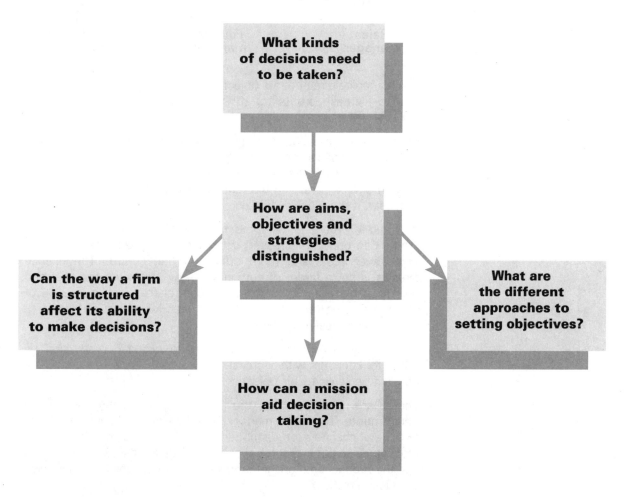

Opening evidence

Marshall Smith Ltd (part 1)

Marshall Smith Ltd makes pine furniture. It has a factory in Wales and its furniture is sold throughout the country by sales representatives who visit furniture stores, take orders and then pass those orders back to the company.

Marshall Smith's management structure looks like this:

The managing director sets objectives for the whole business. Here, it is to increase profits by 20% over the next year. This is the *primary objective*.

He arranges a meeting with the sales director, where they discuss how the sales department can help the business to achieve its primary objective. The sales director agrees a *secondary objective* for the sales department, of increasing the number of units sold by 30% over the next year. If she achieves this increase, she will receive a bonus.

At a similar meeting with the finance director, it is agreed that profits can only be increased if the increased sales are combined with lower costs and more efficient credit control. The finance director is set a target of cutting costs by 10% over the year and putting in place a system of credit control that results in 90% of payments being received within 28 days. Her bonus is dependent on achieving these objectives.

The production director's objective is to increase production by 30%, to keep up with increased sales. Again, he will receive a bonus if he achieves his objective.

There are meetings in the sales, finance and production departments. The sales manager is given the objective of finding two new channels of distribution for the products. The finance manager is to put in place a system for regular chasing of payments and the production manager is to look at new machinery to increase production by 30%.

Organisations that focus too narrowly on achieving only present objectives miss opportunities of uncovering new, more important objectives. Some organisational foolishness – search activity not justified by current objectives – is needed.

Source: BM Bass, *Organisational Decision Making*, Irwin, 1983

But the important decisions, the decisions that really matter, are strategic. They involve either finding out what the situation is, or changing it, either finding out what the resources are or what they should be. These are specifically managerial decisions. Anyone who is a manager has to make such strategic decisions, and the higher his level in the management hierarchy, the more of them he must make.

Source: P Drucker, *The Practice of Management*, Heinemann, 1955

Marshall Smith Ltd (part 2)

Sales director – 'I called a meeting of my sales team and we committed ourselves to doing the 30%. It would mean increasing the number of sales calls by 10% for each sales person, but we said we'd give it a go. The sales manager went out there and found two new wholesalers who would buy our products and I was confident that we would make it.

The next thing I know, I've got one of the wholesalers on the phone, telling me that he received his first consignment of goods on the Monday morning and by the Friday afternoon he had some twit from accounts on the phone, hassling him to pay the invoice. Then I get one of my sales people, from the North, on the line. He was furious that his claim for extra travelling expenses had been queried by the accountants.'

Finance Director – 'It's no good the sales department increasing the number of goods sold if the extra costs are greater than the profit. The sales people go into a customer and promise them the earth if they will buy the goods. It's left to us to try to get money out of them. I'm told to cut costs and the next thing I know, the production department sends me an invoice for £20,000 of machinery. It's ridiculous.'

Production Director – 'It's easy for the sales department. The staff just go out there and get orders in – they can start straight away. We have to be far more organised. My production manager found exactly the right machine and we ordered it for immediate delivery, so that we could cope with the increasing orders. Then accounts ring me up, playing merry hell about the invoice. I am told to increase production by 30% and I do – and what do I get for it?'

1 Deciding what to do – aims, objectives and strategies

Aims and mission statements

Aims

Objectives

Most people have an **aim**. It might be to go to university, or to get a particular job, or it might be to travel around the world. An aim is a long-term target. Once the aim is known, the things which need to be done in order to achieve it must be defined. These are called **objectives**.

For instance, if the aim is to go to university, it will be necessary to gain certain A level grades within a specified time. Some jobs demand specific qualifications or experience. If the aim is to travel, it will be necessary to ensure there are adequate resources available for food, clothing, fares and so on.

After objectives it is necessary to plan the way you are going to achieve them. These are your **strategies**.

If the aim is to go to university, it might be necessary to spend a couple of years at college, devoting the time to A levels and trying to get the best grades possible. An alternative strategy would be to get a job and study in the evenings. If the aim is a particular career, the strategies might be to try to get a job with a particular company, or do some voluntary work to gain experience.

If travel is the aim, it could be achieved by spending a few years working, saving as much as possible and then using that money to finance the trip. Alternatively, it would be possible to acquire skills which would be useful throughout the world and which would then pay for the trip as it proceeded.

Your aim states what you want; your objectives set out what you need to have achieved to get what you want; your strategies are courses of action which enable you to meet your objectives.

Your objectives are determined by your aim, but you have a range of possible strategies. You choose the strategy which seems most likely to be successful – see the example in Figure 2.1.

Figure 2.1 Aims, objectives and strategies

Aim	Go to university to get a Business Studies degree	To be a journalist	To travel around the world
Objectives	• 3 A levels at Grade C or above • A GCSE in a foreign language • Proficiency at basic computing	• 2 A levels at Grade C or above • Ability to take shorthand at 120 wpm • Work experience of journalism	• To have/be able to earn enough money to keep myself for 2 years (say £18,000)
Strategies	• Go to college for 2 years • Get a job and study at evening classes • Get a job that enables me to study part time	• Go to college and study Journalism + A levels • Go to college, study A levels • Go to college, study A levels and get some work experience • Get a junior post in a local newspaper and go to evening classes	• Work for 2 years and save enough to keep me • Go to college and acquire a skill, so that I can work my way around the world

Mission statements

In the same way that people have aims, so do businesses. By law a company must state what it is in business to do. This is its aim and it can be embodied in a **mission statement**.

When one person says 'My mission is to ...' and another person says, 'I would like to ...' we know that each of them has some aim in mind; they each want to do something. But there is a difference between them. We feel that the person who says that she 'has a mission' is more committed to what she wishes to do; she believes in what she wants to do and is prepared to devote herself to achieving her aim. Companies have taken on board this notion of 'mission' and talk about 'having a mission'.

Objectives

The objectives of a business translate the mission statement into specific goals. These objectives state what must have happened in order for the mission to be achieved.

An objective should be specific. For example, 'I really must lose weight' is not really an objective – it is only a rather general hope! An objective would state: 'I will lose 2 lbs each week for the next seven weeks.' I can use this objective to make sure that I have adequate resources (lots of lettuce in the fridge), keep track of how well I am doing (by weighing myself at the end of each week) and to determine when I have succeeded (when I am a stone lighter).

In the same way, a business objective cannot just be, 'To make lots of profits'. A business needs to know exactly how much profit is to be made and by when; it can then make plans for adequate investment. A statement like, 'To make £5,000 profit by the end of the next financial year' is far more useful. Thus an objective is a specific goal, usually quantifiable, and with a timescale.

Primary objectives are the general objectives of the business, such as profit, growth and survival, to which every area or department would subscribe, but in addition to the primary objectives, different areas of the business would have specific, **secondary objectives**.

For example, while a primary objective may be: 'To increase the size of the business by 10% a year over the next 5 years', the Marketing Department has its own, secondary objective, which is: 'To identify new market segments, enabling an extra 10,000 units of production to be sold each year'. This secondary objective, combined with other departments' secondary objectives, enables the business to achieve the primary objective.

Strategies

Strategies are the actions which are taken to achieve goals. There will be a range of possible strategies and the organisation will choose those which it thinks will be the most effective. It will be constrained in its choice of strategies by the resources it has available, the skills of its workforce and the market in which it is operating.

Design for Living's aims, objectives and strategies

Design for Living is an interior design business. It was set up in the 1970s and five years ago moved to its present offices – a coach house in a picturesque Hampshire village.

The aim of Design for Living is summed up in its mission statement: 'To be an imaginative and comprehensive decorating service for the discerning client.'

The things that Design for Living will need to do to achieve its mission are set out in its objectives:

Recession

1 *Financial security* – to have built sufficient security for everyone in the business, so that it can prosper through recessions that last as long as two years. This implies increasing the asset value to £1 million by 1995.

Inflation
Turnover

2 *Growth* – to continue to grow at 20% per annum, or at least 10% more than inflation, to cover the aspirations of everyone in the business. To reach a turnover of £2.2 million by 1992 and then £3.8 million by 1995.

Profits

3 *Profitability* – to increase profitability to 9% net by 1994 and 10% by 1995.

Motivation

4 *People* – to increase the satisfaction, involvement and growth of skills of all staff, appropriate to the needs of the business. Employees should be happy, have the right attitudes and feel part of an effective team.

5 *Business effficency* – to have developed business systems that enable the business to operate at maximum efficiency.

6 *Recognition* – to be recognised by the trade as one of the leading influences in the interior design world.

7 *Succession plans* – to have established succession plans for each of the key personnel so that the business future is not dependent on any one individual or on the partners.

Design for Living's strategies are:

Assets

1 Continue to build the asset base of the company by a continuing programme of investment in new buildings and refurbishment.

Market share

2 Increase turnover by expanding our share of the high quality domestic market.

3 Tighten the management of the business by installing a computerised project management system.

4 Free up the Sales Teams for creative work, promotion and bringing in new business by reducing the time they spend on administration.

IT

5 Ensure that all staff are IT trained, to enable them to use the new systems to forecast and track the profitability of projects.

6 Increase spending on promotion and give specific responsibility for press relations to a senior member of staff.

Job descriptions

7 Produce clear job descriptions for all members of staff, indicating career progression routes. A member of senior management is to be responsible for in-house and external training.

2 Management by objectives

Objectives in action

Some businesses have formal structures for management, which are based on setting objectives. This is known as *management by objectives* (MBO).

In the case study, Marshall Smith Ltd (1) (see opening evidence), the role of the managing director was to set objectives for the other directors, and they then set objectives for their subordinates. The objectives should keep everyone pulling in the same direction – to help the company increase its profits.

Setting objectives enables employees to make decisions. If they are faced with a choice, they can decide what to do on the basis of which action will enable them to meet their objectives. They feel secure because they know exactly what they have to achieve. Achieving clearly set objectives might be linked to bonus payments and act as a motivator.

The objectives are a management tool. They enable management to control the company, by setting objectives for staff and then monitoring whether or not these objectives are met.

That seems to be fine. But as is so often the case, such a straightforward and simple solution can bring problems when decisions are made in isolation.

Objections to objectives

Setting and achieving objectives seems to be a sensible way of co-ordinating a business. But in Marshall Smith Ltd (2) in the opening evidence there is clearly something badly wrong.

Levels of hierarchy

It has been suggested that the problems which Marshall Smith and other companies face in setting and achieving objectives, lie in the structure of business. Traditionally, organisations are hierarchical. The board of directors is at the top of the hierarchy, with senior management, middle management, supervisors and shop floor workers at lower levels.

Certain kinds of decisions are made at different levels in this hierarchy – see Figure 2.2. Important decisions, which affect the whole of the organisation, will be made at board level. If the company is thinking of moving into a new market, with high investment and restructuring, the decision will need to be made there.

Span of control

More routine decisions are made lower down. A departmental manager might make decisions about how to spend her or his department's budget or whether to employ another member of staff. Her or his decisions tend to be confined to her or his area of the business. Lower down still, supervisors and shop floor workers make many decisions on a day-to-day basis.

If someone at a lower level in the hierarchy comes across a problem which requires a major decision, this problem is passed up the chain of command. The decision is then made, and passed back down again. Of course, this structure means that decisions cannot be taken quickly. The whole process takes a great deal of time, but it does allow management to retain control.

MBO is used in an attempt to speed up the decision making process. Instead of decisions being made at the highest level, each layer of management and employees should be in a position to make its own decisions – see Figure 2.2.

Decision making is delegated to people lower down in the organisation. Someone delegates if they give someone else the *power* and *authority* to carry out a task, whilst retaining *responsibility* for the task.

Figure 2.2 Decision making

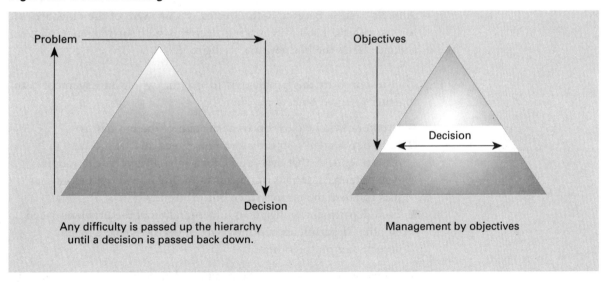

Problem

Decision

Any difficulty is passed up the hierarchy until a decision is passed back down.

Objectives

Decision

Management by objectives

Of course, this means that top management loses some control – they are no longer involved in day-to-day decision making. But, as all decisions are made with reference to objectives which have been set and are monitored by senior management, ultimate control over decision making still rests with them. This constrains the decision making of their subordinates.

In Marshall Smith Ltd decision making was delegated. The problem was that it had become *fragmented*. The employees were given objectives and worked to achieve them. The difficulty was that, in carrying out their objectives, they had no idea of the effect on other areas.

For instance, the sales department had an objective – to increase the number of goods sold. It made a decision to do this by increasing the number of customer visits and finding new outlets. The production department's objective was to increase output, so that sales could achieve its objective. It could not do this without new machinery, so made a decision to invest money in new equipment. The problem was that in order to achieve their individual objectives, sales and production acted in such a way that finance was prevented from achieving its objective. The different departments were acting as quite separate units The decisions made by one department were having a detrimental effect on other departments, resulting in anger and bitterness.

Avoiding a conflict of objectives

It may be that the problems at Marshall Smith Ltd were the result of the way in which the objectives were set. The managing director consulted each director about the appropriate objectives for her or him, but difficulties arose because each director was unaware of the objectives set for the others. Each was making decisions without reference to what anyone else in the business was trying to do.

One response to this problem is to get the whole management team together to agree objectives. Then,

- Everyone will be clear on what the aim of the business is.
- Each department's objectives can be agreed and with other departments, so that everyone knows what everyone else is doing. Any potential conflicts of objectives can be ironed out before they start to affect the performance of the business.
- Each department will gain an understanding of the problems faced by other departments and the effect of decisions made by one department on the others.

The idea is to build teams of committed individuals, who will work together to achieve everyone's objectives. Objectives still act as controls – as constraints on decision making. But a further constraint – the effect of one party's actions on the rest of the business, is added. This further constraint makes the business more efficient. Less time and energy is wasted in conflict.

Recent thinking about objectives

There are far more radical approaches to the question of objectives and some people have gone so far as to suggest that objective setting can, in fact, be counter-productive. Richard Pascale, in his book, *Managing on the Edge*, Penguin, 1990, quotes a Ford senior executive:

> 'Management by objectives is not helpful. We do not want static objectives. We want a process that is obsessed with constantly improving things.'

One problem with setting objectives is that individuals might settle for achieving only that level. They might be capable of doing far more, but as long as their success or failure is determined by whether or not they achieve a certain goal, they have no incentive to go beyond it. Furthermore, the objectives set may be rooted in past needs and performance rather than in the future.

Tom Peters, in *Thriving on Chaos*, Pan Books, 1987, makes this point:

> Performance evaluations, objective setting and job descriptions are three staples of management 'control'. All, though sound of purpose, typically become bureaucratic. They stamp in distinctions and rigidity rather than stamping them out. They impede fluidity.

An advocate of management by objectives would argue that, if you do not give people objectives, they will not know whether what they are doing is right or not. You need objectives to keep everyone moving forward in the same direction. Peters denies this. He goes on to say,

> Control ... is brought about through a shared and inspiring vision, by coaching – and by treating people as fully participating parties.

Instead of spelling out precisely what each person is to do, you make sure that everyone shares a *vision*. This sets out what a company is trying to do and what sort of organisation it is. An employee's objectives are to act in accordance with that vision.

The methods employees can use to bring about the vision are not determined by management. They are encouraged to think for themselves – to experiment – to be entrepreneurial. They can decide what is appropriate, so long as what they do is in keeping with the *values* of the company, which sets out the kinds of behaviour which are considered appropriate.

> Values and trust establish the preconditions that encourage individuals to think, experiment and improve ... Once employees know what an organisation stands for, and believe that it is sufficiently trustworthy to warrant their commitment and effort, they begin to truly extend themselves. If management provides employees with the tools, understanding and latitude to make a difference, great things are possible.
> – Richard Pascale, *Managing on the Edge*, Penguin, 1990

Tom Peters, in his book *Liberation Management*, Macmillan, 1992, emphasises the use of each individual's worth, particularly their brain power, in helping firms to become more efficient, and such a policy excludes 'management decisions' altogether:

> Brain-based companies have an ethereal character compared to yesterday's (1992!) outfits, and that's putting it mildly. Time clocks certainly have no place. And headquarters intrusions had best be rare. (People)....will go where they have to go to add value and do what they have to do to get the job done quickly. Barking orders is out. Curiosity, initiative, and the exercise of imagination are in.

Ford has a statement of vision and values which acts as a 'compass', pointing employees in the right direction.

Ford's vision and values

Mission

Ford Motor Company is a world-wide leader in automotive and automotive-related products and services as well as in newer industries such as aerospace, communications, and financial services. Our mission is to improve continually our products and services to meet our customers' needs, allowing us to prosper as a business and to provide a reasonable return for our stockholders, the owners of our business.

Values

How we accomplish our mission is as important as the mission itself. Fundamental to success for the Company are these basic values:

People – our people are the source of our strength. They provide our corporate intelligence and determine our reputation and vitality. Involvement and teamwork are our core human values.

Products – our products are the end result of our efforts, and they should be the best in serving customers worldwide. As our products are viewed, so are we viewed.

Profits – profits are the ultimate measure of how efficiently we provide customers with the best products for their needs. Profits are required to survive and grow.

Guiding principles

Quality comes first – to achieve customer satisfaction, the quality of our products and services must be our number one priority.

Customers are the focus of everything we do – our work must be done with our customers in mind, providing better products and services than our competitors.

Continuous improvement is essential to our success – we must strive for excellence in everything we do: our products, in their safety and value, and in our services, our human relations, our competitiveness, and our profitability.

Employee involvement is our way of life – we are a team. We must treat each other with trust and respect.

Dealers and suppliers are our partners – the company must maintain mutually beneficial relationships with dealers, suppliers, and our other business associates.

Integrity is never compromised – the conduct of our Company worldwide must be pursued in a manner that is socially responsible and commands respect for its integrity and for its positive contributions to society. Our doors are open to men and women alike without discrimination and without regard to ethnic origin or personal beliefs.

Source: Ford Motor Company

Open Question

Is Ford's mission statement a cynical marketing ploy, or does it represent a genuine attempt to provide a focus for all the company's activities?

One section of Ford's mission statement has been translated into the now famous advertising slogan, 'Everything we do is driven by you.' It is therefore easy to be cynical and suggest that Ford's vision is as much for customer consumption as it is a guiding beacon for employees. After all, in the final analysis, Ford want to sell more cars. On the other hand, if advertising slogans spin off from the mission statement, and more cars are sold as a result, then perhaps the aims are acting precisely as they should in providing a focus for all the company's activities. It is always difficult where ethical issues are concerned to determine whether the business is acting altruistically or as a simple profit maximiser. Doing the right thing, as Marks and Spencer say, is the best way to make profits, but then it may, in the long run, be the *only* way. The argument is circular.

3 Different kinds of decisions

Clearly decisions are made by people at different levels of a business. Not all decisions are of the same kind however, and to an extent they can be categorised.

Programmed and non-programmed decisions

Programmed decisions are the routine decisions which are made in a business every day. For instance, a clerk orders 10 packets of paper for a photocopier when there is only one packet left in her store cupboard. This is a programmed decision, made by an individual, but controlled by the organisation. The company she works for made a decision: how much paper could be ordered when only one packet remained in stock, and the clerk simply implemented that decision. There is a certain procedure to be followed: *Check in the cupboard and when only one packet of paper is left, order another 10 packets.*

Non-programmed decisions are decisions which do not have a formal procedure. They deal with situations which are new and for which there is no established pattern. Individuals who make non-programmed decisions are 'breaking new ground'. They must make the decision themselves and they do not have any precedent to follow.

Of course, most decisions lie somewhere in between. People seldom face totally new situations. Most of the time, a new situation will be very much like an old one, so the rules which applied to the old situation can be modified to apply to the new one.

Tactical and strategic decisions

Frequently made decisions, such as stock ordering, have short term effects. They deal with immediate problems and are predictable. The clerk knows that there are no unforeseen consequences to her ordering the paper – it cannot have a disastrous effect on the company's profits; it is an operating decision concerned with the day-to-day running of the business.

Other decisions are more long-term. For example, a department in a business has to prepare quarterly figures, detailing its costs. These are sent to head office. If the costs are considered too high, the department will be asked to account for the extra expenditure. These decisions are periodic – they happen on a regular basis. They are concerned with the control of a business – head office controlling the expenditure of a department. The sums of money and consequences of a wrong decision are greater than for operating decisions, so these decisions tend to be made by the management of a particular department.

In the end, both the re-ordering of paper and the detailed control of costs are unique parts of the way a company is run. They are called **tactical** decisions. One company will make similar decisions but in an entirely different way to another. Both are equally valid, but they operate within different frameworks or philosophies.

Some decisions are very important and concern the whole of a company. They require considerable expertise and knowledge and carry a high element of risk – the consequences of a wrong decision might be very damaging to the company. These are **strategic** decisions and are usually taken at board level. The acquisition of another company or the restructuring of the business are strategic decisions. They also include decisions to beat your competitors.

4 Decision making and competition

Strategic decision making is different from tactical decision making. A strategic decision maker has her eye on the future. She might make a decision to bear losses in the short term, in order to secure the business in the longer term. Strategy is all about beating the competition.

Innovation

Pricing policies

Patents

VastCo – a suspicious and fictitious company

VastCo produces petrol. Recently, it invented a new kind of petrol – Superfuel – which doubles the number of miles a car can do per gallon. It also reduces wear and tear on the engine and produces far less pollution. It is selling this at a premium price and skimming the market to recoup the huge amount of investment which went into researching and developing the product. Superfuel has to be produced in special refineries, which, although expensive to build, are fairly cheap to run. Unfortunately for VastCo, due to an oversight, the company forgot to patent Superfuel. Upandcoming Industries got hold of the formula and started to produce it themselves. Upandcoming is a much smaller company than VastCo. It used to produce heating oil, but once it got hold of the formula, it concentrated *all* the company's resources into building a refinery and the production and marketing of Upandcoming Superfuel.

VastCo soon found that Upandcoming was taking market share. It could sell the petrol for considerably less than VastCo, because VastCo's price included provision for repaying research and development costs and the huge bill for overheads which such a large company had to pay. Upandcoming was smaller – it had less administration and did not need to spend any money on research and development.

What was VastCo to do?

A board meeting is called at VastCo.

Frederick Ffiendishly–Devious (managing director): 'We've got to do something about Upandcoming. It needs to be taught a lesson. I don't want just to beat it in the petrol market, I want to wipe it out once and for all.'

Marginal cost
Contribution

Olivia Smart (marketing director): 'I've got some figures. The selling price of Superfuel is £3.50 per gallon. The marginal cost is £1.00, repayment of R&D is 50p and £1 is the contribution to overheads. That leaves us with £1 profit on every gallon we sell.'

Ronald Snoop (company spy): 'The Upandcoming figures I've "obtained" are interesting. Their marginal cost is the same as ours, but they have no R&D and their overheads only take 50p. They can sell at £2.50 per gallon and still make £1 profit.'

Frederick Ffiendishly-Devious: 'Right, what we're going to do is slash the price of the petrol to £1.00 a gallon.'

Marjorie Cost (accountant): 'We can't do that. How are we going to get back the R&D costs and who's going to pay the overheads? As for selling Superfuel at no profit at all – have you gone mad?'

Elasticity

Frederick Ffiendishly-Devious: 'Calm yourself! What we'll do is sell Superfuel so that we cover the direct costs of production and break even on the actual production. VastCo has enough reserves to cover the R&D costs, so don't worry about that. The other cost centres in the business can cover the overheads, so we're not actually "losing" money.'

This is what VastCo did. It sold Superfuel for £1.00. Upandcoming lost virtually all its market share. It responded by cutting its price, to £1.50, to cover total costs. This only had a small effect on sales, because its petrol was still 50% more expensive than VastCo.

Upandcoming then cut its price to £1.00, in a desperate attempt to win back market share, but this move was doomed to failure. The company began to lose money, the share price plummeted and VastCo made its move. It offered Upandcoming shareholders a 'fair' price for their shares and acquired the company. The assets which had been 'useless' (the refinery) were incorporated into VastCo and contributed to VastCo's production.

With the competition dealt with, VastCo raised its prices to £4.50 per gallon and soon recouped the money it had "lost" in competition with Upandcoming.

Vastco does not exist of course, but there have been many real-world examples of large companies pricing their product in a way which destroys a new entrant. This has been particularly so in the airline industry. The story of Virgin's attempts to compete on the North Atlantic route is particularly instructive.

Strategic decision making has to be good, because it will give a business the competitive edge. It does not have to be perfect however, as the anecdote below shows.

Fred and Bill were walking in the woods when, suddenly, a bear leaped out from behind a tree and started to chase them.

Both men ran away, as fast as they could. Then Fred looked around. Bill was crouched on the ground, putting on a pair of running shoes.

'For heaven's sake, Bill, what do you think you're doing,' said Fred. 'You don't think that those shoes will help you to run faster than that bear, do you?'

'No,' said Bill, 'but they'll help me run faster than you.'

Goal-seeking organisations

Ansoff, a business theorist, argues that businesses are goal-seeking organisations. They set goals, which they try to achieve through two related processes.

The first is the **logistic** process, which is concerned with taking resources from the environment and producing goods and services, which are then offered back into the environment. For example, labour and raw materials are taken from the environment and finished goods are offered back into the environment.

This logistic process is designed and guided by the second process – the **management** process. This process handles information. The management process has three decision areas: strategic, administrative and operational.

Ansoff's theory is put into action at Kristiana Cosmetics. The company produces toothpaste. Not the normal, mint-flavoured kind, but ecologically friendly, herbal toothpaste.

Originally, it was a relatively small-scale producer and sold its product through health food stores, but it soon decided to increase production and find a high street outlet that would give it access to a larger market.

Kristiana Cosmetics

The board of Kristiana Cosmetics makes strategic decisions: 'We looked at the business as a whole and the decisions we made affect every part of the business. For example, we made the decision that we should go for high volume toothpaste production and move into the high street market. We decided that we would need finance and that retained profits were the best source. If

Retained profits
Sources of finance

retained profits were not available, we would have made the decision about whether or not to approach lenders for finance. The decisions we make are difficult and we often have to make them on the basis of very incomplete data. This is when the experience and expertise of the board members becomes very important.'

Administrative decisions are made by the individual members of the board, in conjunction with their managers. Lara Bowden makes the administrative decisions in the finance department. 'Once the board had made the decision that the finance for the new production equipment was going to be taken from retained profits, it was up to me to look at the financial implications of implementing this decision. I liaised with the production department on the best equipment to buy, from a production and a financial point of view. I worked with marketing to make sure that finance was available for the marketing initiatives which we would need to move from low volume to high volume sales. I had to deal with the inevitable conflicts between strategy and operations – such as the strategic need to increase production against the operational problems of expansion.'

Steve Jackson, the production department manager, makes operating decisions. 'I have to decide how production equipment is going to be set out in the factory. I allocate labour and make sure that there is sufficient stock to keep the line rolling. Everything to do with the physical distribution of the goods is up to me. Most of my decisions are pretty everyday – over a period of time, you make the same decisions over and over. Being "on the shop floor", I don't have time to refer everything up the chain of command, so a lot of the time I have to make decisions "on the hoof". At first, I was worried about this, but, to be honest, none of the decisions I make really has that much effect. It might lose us a few hundred pounds, but nothing horrendous. If I had more time, I suppose that I would make better decisions, but everything always has to be done very quickly and it's more a question of making sure that everything is "good enough" and not striving for perfection.'

Open Question

Why is it important for every job to have non-programmed as well as programmed decisions as part of its specification?

In Ansoff's article, 'Towards a Strategic Theory of the Firm', in *Business Strategy*, Penguin, 1969, he defines the different kinds of problems which a business faces, what the key decisions are and, importantly, who makes those decisions. After all, it is individuals who, in the end, determine the future of a business, and it is to a study of those individuals that we now turn.

Enquiry 3: How can communication aid decision making?

Scope

The first two Enquiries have stressed that decision making is both a process and a skill which must be practised within the context of the organisation's overall aims. To an extent this has played down the role of individuals, and yet people and their contributions are vital to the success of any business. This Enquiry will focus on the roles of individuals, acting either alone or with others in groups, on the way they interact, and on the ways communication can break down, and on how it can be improved.

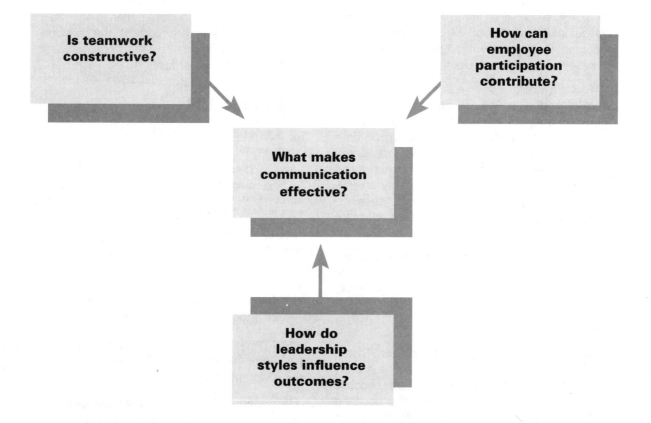

Opening evidence

Plant Packaging

The background

Plant Packaging makes blister packs. It started off as a small, family-owned business, run by the autocratic, but charismatic, Robin Plant.

Plant was recently acquired by Murelle – a large pharmaceutical business. All the Plant employees and managers were retained except for Robin Plant who decided to take early retirement. Plant now packages cough sweets for Murelle.

Plant had suffered from lack of investment and some of its equipment was outdated. Murelle had plans for automating the production line and increasing the range of products which Plant packaged. One reason why Murelle acquired Plant was the highly skilled workforce.

At Murelle, there were regular staff meetings. Murelle had a policy of open management. Decisions affecting the workforce were made by both management and workers. It could be time consuming – information had to be disseminated among so many people and there seemed to be endless meetings and discussion. But it worked – there had been no disputes for over 15 years and the workers often came up with excellent ideas for improvements.

Plant Packaging had a tradition based around Robin Plant's style of management, namely little consultation but clear direction within a pleasant, friendly working environment.

The people

1 Martin Blunt, managing director of Plant. Martin has been with Plant for many years, and he is pleased with Murelle's involvement because they offer the opportunity to invest in updating the machinery in the factory. He sits on the Murelle board.
2 John Fisher, production director of Plant.
3 Harriet Hardwick, production manager of Plant.
4 Sarah Grainer, the personnel manager. Sarah was put into Plant by Murelle and is the only Murelle manager on the site. She wants to put the same decision making process into Plant as she introduced into Murelle. She sees no reason why employees should not participate in decision making. Another 'employee participation' success, similar to the one she engineered at Murelle, and her place on the board will be virtually assured.
5 Tony Batchelor, shop floor supervisor.
6 Liz Powell, shop steward.

On this and the next page are communications between members of the company. Some are part of the formal communication system – memoranda and superiors managing their subordinates. Others are part of the informal communication system – conversations between people, which are not 'official'.

MEMORANDUM

To: John Fisher, production director
From: Martin Blunt, managing director

9 March 1994

AUTOMATION OF PACKAGING SYSTEM
At its next meeting, the board will decide on the new packaging machine we were talking about yesterday. Please prepare a short report, with costs and estimates of revenue figures ASAP.

---

10 March 1994, 9.15 am
John Fisher, production director, talking to Harriet Hardwick, production manager:

'Have you got those brochures on the new packaging machine, Harriet? I need a price for the AS450 model.

'Oh, and can you have a word with Anna-Maria in marketing – I think we were talking about the increase in production upping revenue by £60,000 a year? I need her to verify that.

'Oh, and I want to chat to Sarah in Personnel ...'

10 March 1994, 9.30 am
Tony Batchelor, shop floor supervisor, talking to Liz Powell, shop steward:

> 'Then I heard him say he wanted to see Sarah in Personnel. A new machine and a meeting with Personnel – we all know what that means. Redundancies!'

10 March 1994, 2.00 pm
Sarah Grainer, personnel manager, talking to John Fisher:

> 'Really, we need to get the people who will be using the machine together to make a final decision. They're pretty expert on the shop floor and I would welcome their input. I'll organise it.'

MEMORANDUM

To: Tony Batchelor
From: Sarah Grainer
11 March 1994

STAFF MEETING
Can you get everyone on the shop floor together on Monday 14 March at 15.00?
We've got some decisions to make!

---

11 March 1994, 9.00 am
A conversation between John Fisher, production director, and Harriet Hardwick, production manager:

John Fisher: 'Harriet, have you got those figures yet?'

Harriet Hardwick: 'Here you are. I think you ought to know – there's muttering on the shop floor. I think we ought to tell them what's going on.'

John: 'Not yet. If sales hear that we're getting a quarter of a million to spend on equipment, they'll kick up a hell of a fuss. They'll put in a bid for that new computer system, the board will spend weeks talking about it and we'll not get our machine. No, keep it under wraps until the staff meeting.'

11 March 1994, 9.15 am
Liz Powell: 'Harriet, what's going on?'

Harriet Hardwick: 'Nothing!'

11 March 1994, 9.30 am
Liz Powell speaking to a group of shop floor workers:

> '...then Sarah sends me a memo, asking me to get everyone together on Monday because "We've got some decisions to make." If she thinks she's getting any help from us in deciding who's got to go, she's in for a shock.'

11 March 1994, 10.00 am
A conversation between Harriet Hardwick and John Fisher:

Harriet: 'John, you really are going to have to talk to the people on the shop floor. They want to know what's going on.'

John Fisher: 'I'd rather not. At least, not until the decision has been made. The last thing I want is a great long discussion on which machine we should buy and who should use it. Let's wait for the board meeting and then present it to them as a *fait accompli*.'

MEMORANDUM

To: John Fisher, production director
From: Martin Blunt, managing director

11 March 1994

What on earth's going on down there. Sarah tells me that we've practically got a strike on our hands – why won't they come to the meeting on Monday?

You can either sort this out, or I'll get someone in who can.

Obviously, something has gone very wrong at Plant. On the evidence that you have been given, what do you think the problems are?

1 Decision making in groups

Employee participation in decision making

Employee involvement can operate on a rather simple level, consisting of a willingness on the part of management to listen to ideas coming up from below. Alternatively, it may imply actually creating a role for employees in the decision making process. When this is the case the term **employee participation** is used to describe the process.

Sarah Grainer, the personnel manager of Plant Packaging, wanted to involve employees in decision making. Her first problem was that there was no history of such involvement. Robin Plant, the original owner, did not involve his employees and the corporate culture was not one of employee participation.

Corporate culture

Sarah's attempts to involve the employees met with suspicion, both from the workforce itself, who felt that she was simply trying to steal their ideas, and from Plant management – such as John Fisher – who felt that their authority was being undermined. John seemed to look on the staff and members of other departments as a threat. He wanted to keep the decision making process to himself. He had the information needed to write the report and make the recommendation to the board – perhaps he felt that 'information is power' and disseminating it among the workers reduced his power. If workers are to make real decisions, they need the information – otherwise their involvement is just a sham.

Sarah handled the introduction of employee participation in decision making very badly. She was new at Plant and workers were anxious about her intentions. She had not gained their trust and her actions were easily misinterpreted.

Formal and informal communication

Calling one meeting and asking the workforce what they think is not employee participation. If employees are to be involved, there needs to be a framework for supporting them and formal channels of communication. As there was no history of employee participation at Plant, some training in decision making would be necessary. If the workforce is to be asked to help to contribute to the process, management must ensure that they have the kind of training and knowledge which will enable them to make the kinds of decisions which are needed.

Of course, employee participation does not only refer to companies where the employees are relatively unskilled or less educated than the management. It is as relevant to companies where the employees are highly educated and skilled. Employee participation in decision making means that decisions will be made by groups of people, so decision making has to be adapted to this different method of working.

Why make decisions in groups?

There are clear advantages to working in groups. A large group of people has a greater pool of skills and knowledge and if every employee in the company feels involved in decision making, they are more likely to make sure that the decisions are implemented and work successfully.

Of course group working does not mean that every time there is a decision to be made, the *whole* workforce will gather together to look at the pros and cons of the proposal, because that is impractical and unwieldy. Likewise there are disadvantages to decision making by groups, if they are large. Often, the sheer numbers involved mean that decisions take far too long to be made or the groups fragment into smaller ones. If this happens informally and without control, these small groups can end up arguing with each other and making no progress.

Quite obviously, the larger the group, the more difficult is the communication between members. In smaller groups, it is easier to make sure that everyone is involved in the discussion.

Communication between groups is as important as communication between individuals within a group. Figure 3.1 shows different types of *communication networks*.

Figure 3.1 Communication networks

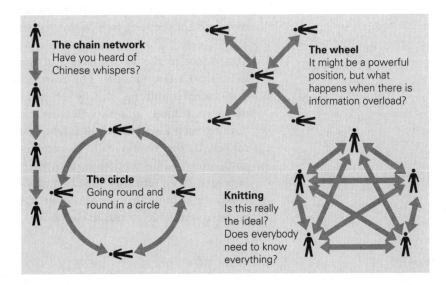

The chain network
Have you heard of Chinese whispers?

The wheel
It might be a powerful position, but what happens when there is information overload?

The circle
Going round and round in a circle

Knitting
Is this really the ideal? Does everybody need to know everything?

Open Question

What are the advantages and disadvantages of each kind of communication network?

In most organisations, employees who want to be involved in decision making will be members of small groups – perhaps devoted to addressing one particular problem. Each group must have a clear *task* – it must know exactly *what* it is supposed to be deciding about and *why* the decision is necessary.

The group needs an **action schedule**. Individuals in the group will need to know what their function is in the decision making process. This will depend on their skills and capabilities. Some people are very good at creative thinking, but hopeless when it comes to organising things. Other people are happy dealing with figures and quantitative information. Either a natural leader will emerge from the group, or someone will have to be appointed. The role of the leader will not be to make the decision, but to ensure that everyone has a fair chance to contribute and make sure that the group does not stray from its task. The leader also needs to make sure that everyone knows when the meetings will be and where. She or he will often have to liaise with other leaders, to make sure that everyone in the company is aware of what is going on at individual meetings.

There will be *interaction* between members of the group. This will be **verbal** – discussion, argument, conflict – or body language which is **non-verbal**. It might be *rational* – with clearly thought out arguments – or *emotional* – the expression of feelings.

Some companies have set up **quality circles** – groups of employees who meet to make decisions about how their company can improve the way it does things. This idea was imported from Japan where it had been highly successful, and it is seen as a central part of that style of management known as **Japanisation** – the adoption of Japanese management thinking into Western organisations.

Unfortunately the vast majority of quality circles do not survive for more than a few months. The reasons why this is so vary. It could be that there is still no history of genuine employee participation in decision making, and also because no help or training is given to develop such a culture. Or it might be that management, which is also unused to the system, fails to recognise that to be a success quality circles need to be supported, and their decisions acted upon or at the very least taken seriously. Finally it may be that methods which work in Japan are simply inappropriate in the different cultural and social environment which exists in the West.

Teamwork and successful groups

It is difficult to say what makes a *successful* group. Jon Katzenbach and Doug Smith looked at *teams* – groups of people who work together successfully. A group becomes a real team when it consists of '... a small number of people with complementary skills who are committed to a common purpose, performance goals and an approach for which they hold themselves mutually accountable.' – Katzenbach and Smith, 'The Wisdom of Teams', *Harvard Business Review*, 1993.

Katzenbach and Smith looked at groups of people who work together. The least effective is the **working group**, which is nothing more than a collection of individuals. The quality of the work of that group is no greater than the quality of work of each of the individuals – there is nothing gained by their working in a team.

Then there is the **pseudo-team** – where each person actually performs worse because they are part of that team. Perhaps there is some confusion about what the team's goals are, or there are personality clashes.

A **potential team** is a collection of individuals, who are trying very hard to work together. They do not succeed, not because they are a bad team, but because the task they have been given is unclear or because they lack discipline.

Katzenbach and Smith argue that organisations are full of these *potential teams* – people who have the potential to become members of high performance teams. The company needs to support these potential teams – give them stimulating and worthwhile tasks to do and appropriate training, so that they can become *real teams*, whose performance exceeds the performance of the individual members. A real team adds value to employees' creativity and skills.

The Japanese approach

Some Japanese companies have adopted a slightly different approach to group decision making. They use a system called *ringiseido*.

Here is the situation. A decision is required on a problem. Everyone in the line concerned with that decision is asked about it. Each person writes their solution down and passes it to the person above them. There is no judge and jury. No one is required to say 'This is a good idea' or 'This is a bad idea'. Instead, each person adds their information to the proposal so that, by the time it reaches the top of the chain, the decision has practically made itself. The people who will have to carry out the decision are involved from the beginning. If a decision is made which will be problematic to implement, at least everyone knows who thinks it will be problematic and why.

In the West, the people who make the decisions are often different from the people who have to carry them out. Decision making can be speedy as a result, but the implementation of the decision can be slow and problematic. In the Japanese model, the decision takes longer to make, but, once made, can be implemented more efficiently.

Open Question

Why are many UK managers lukewarm about, or positively against, employee participation?

Employee participation is found more often in continental Europe, especially Germany, than it is in the UK. One of the implications of the European Single Market is that businesses will all be required to provide for a degree of employee participation. This was one reason why the UK government had reservations about the Maastricht Agreement.

2 Management styles and decision making

Task and people management

Managers have two functions. Their **task** function relates to what they have to get done – the projects to be completed, the products to be manufactured. It is also concerned with initiating and directing – telling their staff what to do and making sure that they do it. A manager also has a **human** function. This is keeping the group happy, encouraging staff and settling disputes.

Motivation

Managers usually try to make a compromise between the task and the human aspects of their roles. Sometimes the task is more important and at other times the human side is emphasised. A good manager knows which to emphasise and when.

The task and human aspects of decision making

Look at the people you live or work with. Who is good at their task function? Who is not very popular but respected because they are good at their job? Who can motivate people to do something, even though they may not be brilliant at actually doing it themselves?

Looking at the task and human aspects of the decision, what would you do if:

■ The financial report had to be at head office by the end of the day and at 4 pm one of the accounting staff wanted to go home early because he had a headache ...

- A shop floor worker comes to you, claiming that she simply cannot continue to work with the supervisor. She is cagey about the reasons and is reluctant to return to her post. If she does not return within the hour, the production line will have to be stopped ...
- You have forgotten to put together a report, which is needed for the board meeting the next day. You need input from three members of your staff and it is already 6 pm. They are putting on their coats, ready to go home ...
- It is Friday lunchtime and your secretary has gone out to lunch to celebrate someone's birthday. He has been gone an hour and a quarter and you have a letter to be word processed ...

Leadership

In any organisation, you get leaders. Sometimes these are officially appointed, like a colonel in the army; at other times, they emerge from a group, like the ringleader in a gang. Leaders do not all act in the same way – they have different leadership styles and the style which a leader adopts has a great influence on the way in which decisions are made in a group.

The democratic leader

The democratic leader emphasises an interpersonal style of management. He does not rely on a formal structure for decision making. He does not call meetings and issue papers. Instead, he gets out of his office and talks to his staff. He involves them in the decision making process and is not so aloof that he makes decisions and then imposes them on everyone else. He is pleased that he cannot walk along a corridor without being stopped several times for chats with members of staff. When he is in his office, the door is always open and anyone can drop by and speak to him without an appointment. On the face of it this style of leadership would appear to be very popular with staff, but there can be problems.

One is that there never seems to be a point when a decision is made. Decisions just tend to emerge, and some staff feel totally excluded. There is no formal structure to inform people about the issues which are being discussed – only those involved know what the current concern is. It's more a question of 'being in the know' about what is going on than being informed. The leader is the only one who is aware of everything that is going on and who has all the information. Everyone else just has fragments which they glean from their conversations with him. Of course, if this is what happens, then the leadership is only superficially democratic.

Open Question

What are the features of a genuinely democratic leader?

Another democratic approach is, in contrast, to have very open meetings with everyone invited, and open debate. The problem here is that it does not necessarily suit some people to have such an open forum, and there may be a feeling that the results are in some way or other 'rigged' by the manager.

Source: *Financial Times,* 25 April 1994

The autocratic leader

Not all managers even try to involve their employees in decision making. They believe that their role is to make decisions and then to convey those decisions to their staff. They have an authoritarian management style.

Authoritarian managers are not necessarily unpleasant people. After all, not all staff want to be involved in decision making. Perhaps they look on their jobs as no more than a way of earning money and they get their personal satisfaction elsewhere. There are plenty of people who have dead-end, boring jobs, but absorbing hobbies. Authoritarian managers suit these people. They will make the decision and bear the responsibility. The employees simply carry out the tasks they are required to do, with no blame attached if things go wrong.

Authoritarian managers do not necessarily want confrontation, because they might lose. It is far better to avoid confrontation and so avoid the risk of being beaten.

Such managers can exclude subordinates from decision making without necessarily being unpopular. In fact, they are often respected because of their ability to make decisions and shoulder responsibility. But for some, particularly the ambitious subordinate who craves a degree of decision making, this can be exasperating. Discussion is excluded and talk is a one-way flow – from the manager downwards. The subordinate is only allowed to respond to the manager, not to initiate.

The need to avoid confrontation often leads authoritarian managers to surround themselves with people who will not argue with them or their decisions. The problem then is for people who recognise that the right decisions are not getting made, to get their ideas across. Since there are no open, public channels for getting involved in decisions, a network of informal channels of communication and influence has to be created.

The pendulum approach

Of course there are other leadership styles besides democratic and autocratic, and no leader ever falls neatly within one category all the time. In the armed forces, for instance, it might be assumed that an autocratic style would prevail, but that is not the case.

Officers are taught that the leadership style has to be appropriate for the circumstances. If an Exocet missile is heading towards the ship it would not be right for the captain to gather a group together and arrive at a consensus for action. Instead he makes a decision and expects, and gets, immediate obedience. On the other hand, if an officer requires subordinates to perform a difficult, dirty or dangerous job it may be entirely appropriate to allow discussion and debate. In the end any orders will be obeyed, but an officer will know that the individual who has to carry out the task will be far better motivated, and thus do the job better, if he or she is consulted beforehand.

This style of leadership can be described as like a clock pendulum – see Figure 3.2. The best sort of leader is one who is able to identify the most appropriate style for the prevailing circumstances. As Victor Vroom wrote: 'It makes more sense to talk about participative and autocratic situations than to talk about participative and autocratic managers.' – Quoted in D. S. Pugh and D. J. Hickson, *Writers in Organisations*, 4th edition, Penguin, 1989.

Figure 3.2 Pendulum leadership

3 Company structures and decision making

Effective communication

The formal organisation of a company can either help or hinder communication, but it is not just *how* information is passed up and down the chains of command and across the organisation that matters. It is vital that the communication which supports the decision making should be *effective* communication.

Creativity and motivation

'I run a fairly small division of a large company. We work together as a team and it can be very creative. We had been working on a voice controlled robot during our free time. It was going well, but we soon found that we could not go on without better resources.

'So we put together a proposal, asking the parent company for the resources we needed to continue the development work. We were hauled before a panel of all the big-wigs in the company and told to present our case. It was worse than being in court.

'Anyway, it did not go that well. The panel were suspicious and very critical and there was a gremlin in the works that day. The robot whizzed around, crashed into furniture then came to a halt in the corner of the room, where it buzzed and beeped and wouldn't move. What we wanted was resource to develop the project and iron out problems, but they wouldn't listen.

'I felt awful. I had persuaded my people to take this project to the parent company, but the people who could make a decision treated us like children. Instead of being supportive and finding out from us what the robot could do and what the prospects for future development were, they really didn't want to try anything different.

'We went back to our division very disheartened. We will work on the robot ourselves, in our own time, but this is the last time I will try anything different with the parent company. We'll just keep developing the boring, mundane things they want to see and keep the exciting stuff to ourselves.' – Dave Matten, divisional director

The fact that people from one part of a business are talking to people from another part, or that superiors are talking to their subordinates, does not mean that real communication is taking place.

Communication in business does not just involve passing on information. Often, it is concerned with arguing, persuading, coaxing. If you are trying to get someone to do something, you use arguments which will persuade them.

The person who is asking for something will present their plan in the most favourable light. They may well gloss over problems, being unwilling to discuss them openly in case it prejudices the decision. Evidence is presented in the most flattering way and ideas which do not have a good chance of being accepted may not even be put forward. Subordinates ask superiors for things which they believe the superiors will be willing to give.

On the other hand, superiors try to get their subordinates to come up with ideas, to be creative and to take risks. When the subordinates don't, the superiors wonder why. Perhaps it is because it is safer not to take risks. If you have put time and energy into a project, as Dave's team had, and that project is torn apart by a group of people who have failed to understand it, the reaction is inevitable.

Corporate culture

Sometimes organisations work together to come up with ideas and to make decisions about how to develop them. Other organisations have a different culture. There, innovation comes about in spite of the organisation, not because of it. The organisation is excluded from decision making because it stifles creativity.

> **Compare these two views: which one is 'right'?**
>
> 'We need an organisational structure which will support the creativity of its employees. People need to be encouraged to take risks and to develop ideas. There will be mistakes and companies need to accept that. It is the price they must pay.' – product development director
>
> 'But you can't let employees do what they like. If you do, you end up with fragmented groups, working on pet projects, with no overall control or coherence. Someone has to take a decision about what will and what will not happen in a business and the best people to do it are the board. If someone's idea is a good one, it will pass muster with the board. If it does not, then it was not a good idea and should not be developed anyway.' – board director

Company structures in an uncertain world

Tom Peters, the management writer, has examined companies which are consistently successful. His conclusion is that the modern world is changing so fast that it is almost impossible to make predictions about the future.

Change management

Successful companies do not try to predict the future; rather, they structure themselves so that they can respond to changes as and when they happen.

As the managing director of a division of a computer company once said: 'Some businesses are like the QE2; others are like fleets of dinghies, sailing in formation. If I'm sailing straight across the Atlantic, I'd rather do it in the QE2 than in a dinghy. But if I had to keep changing direction I'd rather be the captain of a fleet of dinghies than of the QE2!'

Small companies, Peters argues, can respond quickly to change. They usually have short chains of command – decisions can be made and implemented faster. They are often more specialised. They are at the leading edge in their field. Staff are experts and the business is very close to its market.

Economies of scale

Big companies are slower. But there are advantages to being big: economies of scale. Just because an organisation is big it does not mean it will not be creative, but it can be cumbersome, and as Dave Matten found (page 56), it can stifle innovation. Robert Heller in *The Decision Makers*, put it more graphically:

> 'It isn't just a question of the super-corporation finding it difficult to formulate new initiatives: it will crush any that somehow arise, and sometimes do it inadvertently, like a large sow rolling over and squashing a piglet to death.' – Robert Heller, *The Decision Makers*, Hodder & Stoughton, 1989

Organisational structures

Perhaps the answer is to be a big company, but divided into smaller units. Each unit can be as responsive as a small company, but keep the benefits of size. Peters says that businesses will have to 'be big' but 'act small'. They will depend on highly skilled, creative, flexible workers, who are partners with the firm and share in the decision making. The days of unskilled workers, directed by managers, will be over. People from different areas in the company will have to work together and learn to see problems from a 'whole company' perspective.

This has profound implications for the entire decision making process. In many companies, the workers 'have' the problem (or 'are' the problem!) and management 'solves' the problem. It is assumed that the workers cannot solve it themselves. Peters rejects this view.

> 'It's absurd! We don't want for evidence that the average worker is capable of moving mountains – if only we'll ask him or her to do so, and construct a supportive environment.' – Tom Peters, *Thriving on Chaos*, Pan Books, 1987

Honda believes that most problems are the result of inefficient systems, not inefficient workers. The company's motto is, 'To lead is to serve' – management leads by enabling the workers to do their jobs.

Pascale, in his book *Managing on the Edge,* quotes a Ford manager describing his boss:

> 'He is an enabler. He doesn't make a lot of decisions. When you bring a quarrel to him, he'll say, "You two go off and see if you can't figure that out. Have dinner, have lunch – don't just write memos. Get your people together. Give me the alternatives, but see if you can't work something out."' – Richard Pascale, *Managing on the Edge*, Penguin, 1990

Enabling people

If you enable people, the change can be startling. The following example is taken from the experience of visiting a car assembly plant organised by Japanese management.

'From the front of the line, the voice of the guide droned on, discussing the quality of the material-handling system, robotics, innovative painting, etc. But I had lost interest. I was fascinated by the workforce. I kept comparing them with my familiar world in the assembly plants in Flint, Michigan. What had they done to these people to make them care like this?

Now we were in the middle of the body shop watching a group of four men in an assembly operation. Several of the visiting GM (General Motors) managers had lagged behind the rest of the tour group to watch these men work.

'Have you ever seen anything like it?' marvelled one. 'Look at 'em go!'

'How do they train each other? Remember, isn't that what they told us?'

'Yeah, but check that equipment. It's probably an act. There's no way in hell those guys could keep this pace up all day. They probably pick up speed every time they take a tour through their area.'

One manager turned to another. 'You know, I couldn't do that job with fewer than six men in my plant.'

'You gotta give these Japanese credit,' the other said. 'How could they get those suckers to design their own work processes? And with no experience?'

They continued to watch in silence for another few minutes. The men before them never let up their pace. Finally, the plant manager could stand it no longer. He clapped his hands as he stepped out from behind his hiding place.

'Bravo!' he yelled at the workers. 'You guys are something else! If only I could have people like you!'

The workers turned and smiled at the men as they left, but I lingered behind to hear their reaction. One of them turned and said to the others: 'It's too bad, isn't it, that they don't realise that they already have people like that.'

Source: Richard Pascale, *Managing on the Edge*, Penguin, 1990

Delayering

One of the ways in which firms are enabling people is by changing the organisation's structure. By flattening out their hierarchies, businesses are forcing decision making to lower levels because it is physically impossible for managers to monitor such wide spans of control.

This has huge implications for training. Putting people in the position of having to make decisions is not enabling, unless they are equipped to perform this role. If they are not, they are likely to become demotivated rather than the opposite.

This meshes with the somewhat obvious, but often ignored fact that the public image of a company is made or destroyed by employees much further down the hierarchy than is often believed by those at the organisation's apex. For instance, if someone stays in a hotel, the image which that hotel projects, and the chance of the guest returning or not, may well rest with the person who cleans the room, or the waiter at breakfast, rather than with the manager, with whom the guest is most unlikely to come into contact.

Employees are generally very aware of the vertical structure of the company for which they work. They know its pecking order – the hierarchy. The public are much more interested in the horizontal layer – the one with which they have the most contact. It is often quite far down the hierarchy, but the employees there can make or break the company's image and hence have a profound impact on its profitability. This is illustrated in Figure 3.3.

Figure 3.3 Company image

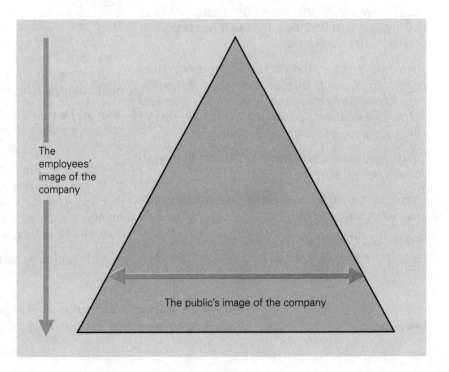

The employees' image of the company

The public's image of the company

The notion of giving people more and more responsibility in an enlightened and forward thinking business environment may work for the very few, of course. It is just as likely that the organisation's structure actually works against such ideas.

The 'laws' of organisational stupidity – just for fun

Most people have heard of Parkinson's First Law, which states that 'Work expands to fill the time available.' There are other laws of organisational stupidity.

Professor Jerry Harvey's Abilene Paradox states that: 'People in groups agree on decisions which, as individuals, they know are stupid.'

Another is Macaulay's Buckshifter. He insists that: 'Initiative declines with increasing ease of communications.'

Professor Chris Argyris, from Harvard University, argues that we respond to any problem which threatens to land us in hot water by first finding a way to by-pass it. We then cover up the by-pass and find a way of covering-up the cover-up ... and so on. As a result, the problem not only fails to be solved, it is not even admitted to exist – it becomes 'undiscussable'.

Hence Argyris's Archetype says: 'The more threatening a problem to those responsible for solving it, the deeper it will become ingrained under ramifying layers of camouflage'.

Argyris's Archetype explains the Buckshifter. With high-speed communications, people who are faced by risky decisions can easily pass them upwards to their superiors. It also explains the Abilene Paradox. People in groups will agree to what they know, individually, is stupid, because the wiser courses of action which need to be taken to solve a problem have become undiscussable. No one dares mention them, for fear of losing their job.

The following quote may sound familiar: 'I work for a small company, started by a charismatic, but erratic owner 20 years ago. It is profitable, but chaotic. The problem is that we set up systems for getting things done, but the owner then by-passes the systems to get things done quickly. This causes havoc. We then have a meeting to look at how the system should be changed. We spend ages tinkering with the system, when the real cause of the problem is the owner!'

4 Chaos and conflict

The drawbacks of consensus

So far, it has been assumed that one of the most important aspects of decision making is gaining the commitment of a whole team to a decision. Mission statements and objective setting are ways of getting people to work together towards a single goal. Underlying everything so far is the assumption that consensus is a good, even a necessary, thing.

Consider the following situation, however.

> Three men are out in a boat.
>
> 'As I see it,' said the first man, 'the problem is that our feet are going to get wet. Does everyone feel that their feet are getting wet?'
>
> 'Yes, I think we can all go along with that,' said the second. 'Whenever our feet have got wet before, we've all needed dry socks. Shall I see what I can do about socks?'
>
> 'Yes, that's a good idea. And shoes, too,' added the third. 'Don't forget about the shoes. Can we all agree that I should get the shoes?'
>
> 'I think that's carried,' said the first man. 'You'll see to socks and you'll see to shoes. I'll keep a check on the depth of the water.'

This ought to be excellent decision making. The problem is clear – everyone agrees what it is. A decision is made, which is agreed unanimously.

The trouble is that everyone's feet are getting wet because *the boat is sinking*! Everyone is so tied up with the process of agreeing on decisions that no one has noticed what's really going on!

Richard Pascale, in *Managing on the Edge*, Penguin, 1990, argues that too much agreement and unanimity is a very dangerous thing for a business. He suggests that businesses can easily become narrow in their vision and complacent. Everyone *agrees* what the problems are; everyone *agrees* about the causes; everyone *agrees* about what should be done. The problem, Pascale says, is that everyone is so busy agreeing that no one sees what the real trouble is.

The company mindset

It is not just 'happy, unanimous' organisations which suffer from this problem. Some organisations have a certain philosophy – a particular way of looking at things and doing things which becomes a rather static and sterile mindset. Pascale examined the Ford Motor Company.

The Ford Motor Company

It was the early 1980s and Donald Petersen had just become President of Ford. His mission was to turn the company around. The company had real problems. On the production front – emphasis was on high volume, regardless of quality. The design team was disheartened – any innovative ideas were rejected. Management seemed more concerned with internal politics than dealing with the real problems of the business. Ford had become a huge bureaucracy.

In 1987 Ford broke all previous industry records for profitability. How did it manage this almost miraculous transformation?

Ford began by 'shaking up' the organisation. The assembly line had been very traditional, with workers assigned to specialised tasks and a rigid hierarchy. No assembly line worker expected to be involved in decision making. There was a clear hierarchy – problems were passed up and decisions were, eventually, passed down.

Ford expanded its Employee Involvement programme. Shop floor workers were encouraged to make suggestions about how production could be improved. One employee said: 'Working at Ford in the early eighties was like participating in a social revolution. There was a tremendous upwelling of initiative from the ranks. Somehow we channelled it constructively.'

Similar changes were made to management. Many problems were caused by misunderstandings and disagreements between departments in the company. Departments simply did not talk to each other – it was looked on as 'meddling' and frowned on. Conflict was avoided because there was no way to control it.

Cross-company meetings were called and people began to talk and argue. Conflicts rose to the surface, but the meetings provided a safe forum for healthy conflict management. By presenting their ideas openly and having to defend them, management realised their strengths and weaknesses. Conflict was positive.

Source: Adapted from Richard Pascale, *Managing on the Edge*, Penguin, 1990

Open Question

What is the role of the mission statement (pages 38–9) in the changes at Ford?

The same is true of groupwork in school or college. There are always group dynamics. Is the *best* work done when everyone agrees? It is easy to mistake having the easiest time for doing the best work! It is vital to look at the quality of the output, not how much everyone enjoys the process.

Conflict can then be healthy in business. The trick is to manage conflict so that employees do not feel threatened and disheartened.

Now that we have looked at how organisations go about making decisions, we can consider the *tools* which are available to help them.

Enquiry 4: How can outcomes be analysed?

Scope

A jury at a trial can only make a judgement of guilt or innocence on the basis of the evidence presented – the greater its weight, the less likely it is that an incorrect decision will be made. The same is true of business decision making: the better the evidence, the less the likelihood of error. The parallel cannot be taken too far, however. Whilst a jury seeks the truth about a past event, managers are trying to frame a policy for the future. Clearly data are invaluable in this regard, and models have been developed which use statistical techniques in order to clarify thinking. For a number of reasons such models must be treated with caution, not least because they refer to past events and situations which can never be identical to those which will prevail in the future.

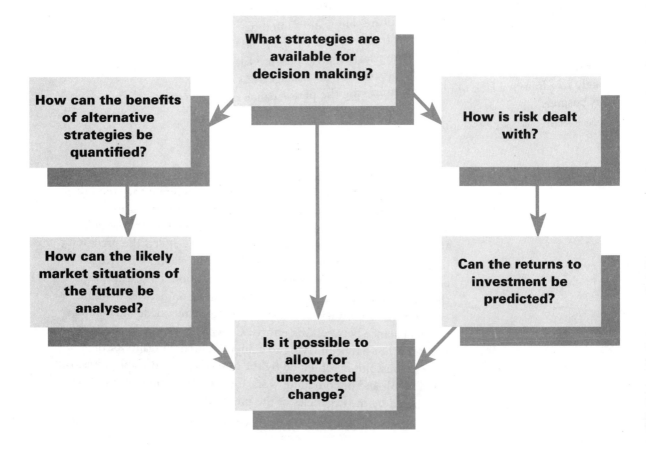

Opening evidence

'Nothing ventured, nothing gained.'

'You never know what will happen in the future. In business, you have to make plans for the future *now*, so you are always thinking about what that future might be like.'

This radical management thinker continued to hold monthly meetings with his managers, but not for the usual hashing over of the historic figures. His questions were never about the past or the present, but only about creating the future. How, he wanted to know, are you going to improve your business, area by area, and what will be the results if you do? The psychological pressure for business creativity was built into the process: for no manager was likely to admit to a lack of plans for improving the performance of his business.

Source: Robert Heller, *The Decision Makers*, Coronet, 1989

To make the present business effective may require one specific course of action. To make the future of the business different may require different action. Yet what is done to make the present business effective inevitably commits resources, inevitably moulds the future. What is done to anticipate the future inevitably affects the present business in all its policies, expectations, products, and knowledge efforts. Major actions in every one of the economic dimensions have therefore to be consistent with one another. Conflicts between the conclusions of the various analyses have to be reconciled. There has to be a balance between the efforts. Otherwise, one effort undoes what another has been trying to achieve. The hard reality of the present must not be obscured by the lure of tomorrow's promises. But the difficult and discouraging work for tomorrow must also not be smothered by the urgencies of the present.

Source: Peter Drucker, *Managing for Results*, Heinemann, 1964

In many decisions, including investment ones, a number of studies show that hopes, wishes and internal politics play an important part. The element of uncertainty enables expectations of the results of the decision to be biased in accordance with wishes. Cost estimates, for instance, may be too optimistic. Some of these biases may be unconscious; others may be consciously manipulated by managers who want a particular decision to be taken. One study even reports the following statement: 'In the final analysis, if anybody brings up an item of cost we haven't thought of, we can balance it by making another source of saving tangible.'

Source: Rosemary Stewart, *The Reality of Management*, Pan, 1963

Great decision makers, like chess grandmasters, don't make the move that yields the greatest immediate advantage, but the move which, many steps later, will give them the best, the overwhelming position.

Source: Robert Heller, *The Decision Makers*, Coronet, 1989

All uncertainty is fruitful ... so long as it is accompanied by the wish to understand.

Source: Antonio Machado, *Juan de Mairena*, 1943, tr. Ben Belitt

It comes as no surprise that the Japanese are much better in approaching the future than many British firms. They make great use of mathematical models, which are then discussed at length among many managers. But German and US companies are also advanced in the use of scenarios. Proof of the viability of the Shell approach is the Gulf War. How did that affect Shell? 'Not a great deal at all,' says Mr Kahane — head of socio-political, economic and technological planning for Shell International. 'None of our scenarios had involved such a violent clash, but we had considered a situation in which there was serious disruption to oil supplies in the Gulf. Whether this came by war, or an accident, or by religious fundamentalism did not really matter to us as the net effect is the same.'

Source: Adapted from Paul Miller, 'Scenarios make the future feel familiar', *Independent on Sunday*, 24 March 1991

1 Dealing with risk

Cashflow

All decisions are about the future and organisations have to make estimates about future cashflows and profits. These estimates are quantitative – they are expressed in numbers. But using numbers can be more problematic than might be imagined.

A cold calculation

A pharmaceutical company has been doing research and it believes that it has found a cure for the common cold. The cure is in its earliest stages and the company wishes to know whether or not it should proceed.

It has commissioned market research, which indicates that it could make £20 million profit from the drug (£22 million – £2 million development costs).

Its research and development people need £2 million to continue their work. On past experience the company calculates there is a 50/50 chance that this continued research will result in the successful development of the product.

If the business chooses to invest the £2 million in research and development, it could gain £20 million. However, there is a possibility that the research might fail and the £2 million would be lost.

Given a 50/50 chance of success, this could be expressed as:

   'We could have £20 million, but with only a 50% chance of getting it.'

Or:

   '£20 million × the 50% chance of getting it = £10 million.'

£10 million is not what the company will make – it is not a real sum of money which they might never have. It is simply shorthand for saying:

   '£20 million, with a 50% chance of getting it.'

Probability

When a business has to choose between options, its decision will be made by looking at the outcomes of each and choosing the best. Some outcomes are more likely than others – they are less risky. One way of talking about risk is to express it in terms of probability. Something which is very risky has a low probability; something which is more certain has a higher probability. The pharmaceutical company has simply expressed the outcomes of its decisions in such a way that the risk is included.

If something is certain, it has a probability of one. It is certain that people will still be using computers in business tomorrow. If something is impossible, it has a probability of zero. It is impossible (or so unlikely as to be discounted) that every business in Britain will go bankrupt tomorrow. Sometimes it is easier to express these probabilities as percentages. Something which has a 0% probability is impossible; something which has a probability of 100% is certain.

Probability can also be applied to non-quantitative decisions. No one can be absolutely certain what the future will be like, but some things are pretty sure. It is very probable that there will not be a revolution in Britain tomorrow; it is very improbable that the Loch Ness monster will be caught next week.

Some improbable events?

- the Labour Party winning the next General Election
- a cure for AIDS being found within the next five years
- a settlement being built on the moon
- personal computers being sold for £25.00 each

What estimate would you give of the probabilities of the above?

What did you look at when deciding on these probabilities?

The idea of probability is used in many different ways by businesses, but it is especially important when choices have to be made between alternatives.

2 Choosing between alternatives: decision trees

A technique for decision making which combines the approach used in *issue diagrams* with a way of quantifying the benefits to be gained from different possible decisions is called a **decision tree**.

Life challenges

Anna has just taken her GCSEs and she is thinking about whether to get a job straight away, or go to college. She has been looking at the local newspaper and although there are some jobs, the situation is pretty bleak.

If she goes to college, she would be better qualified, so she should find it easier to get a job. She might even be able to go on to university, which should improve her chances even more. Before she can make a decision, she needs a clear way of setting out the alternatives and clarifying her thinking.

Figure 4.1 College or a job?

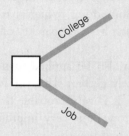

Her first decision is between going to college and getting a job. She draws a square, as a decision point, with the two possibilities coming off it (Figure 4.1).

She does not know whether she will be successful at finding a job, so she draws a **node** (circle), for an unknown outcome at the end of the job line, adding the possibility of either success or failure. Equally, she does not know if she will be a success or a failure at college, so she draws another node at the end of that line.

If she is successful at college, she can decide whether to get a job or go to university. She draws a **decision point** at the end of the success line, with university or job as the things she must decide between. If she chooses university, she does not know if she will be successful there, so she indicates another unknown outcome.

Figure 4.2 A decision tree

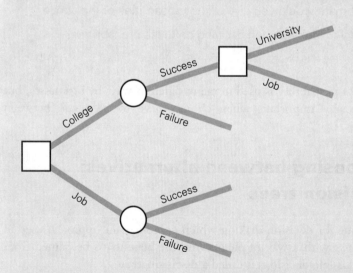

Anna has drawn a **decision tree** (Figure 4.2). She can see all the points where decisions have to be made (squares) and where there are unknown outcomes, nodes. The problem is that she has nothing on the decision tree to help her to decide between alternatives. For that task it seems reasonable to use the different salaries, which she might earn as the consequences of her decisions.

In the local newspaper, there are jobs for school leavers. The lowest salary she has seen is about £6,000. She has read about school leavers who are earning £20,000. She decides to put £6,000 as the worst possible salary and £20,000 as the best she could get if she leaves school and gets a job straight away.

A friend of hers left college with poor A levels and got a job. She is earning £10,000 a year, so Anna decides on this figure as the outcome of failure at college. Another friend left college with good A levels and is working for £12,000 a year, so Anna puts this figure as the outcome for a job after college.

As a successful business studies graduate, Anna would expect to earn £20,000 a year. If she is not successful in her degree, she reckons that she might have to settle for £10,000 a year. Copy and complete Figure 4.3 with the information given above. Note that the university option requires a node for an unknown outcome.

Figure 4.3 Developing the decision tree

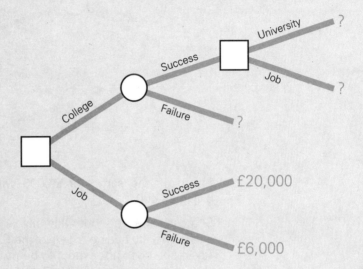

With these figures on her decision tree, Anna considers her position. The decision tree seems to point to leaving school, getting a good job and earning £20,000 a year. Surely it cannot be so easy?

No, Anna realises that the chances of earning £20,000 a year at 16 are very slim indeed. She might manage it, but it is unlikely. At best, she estimates that she has a 10% chance of doing this, but she has a 90% chance of having to settle for £6,000 a year. She may not know the outcome of looking for a job at 16, but she can make a fair estimate of the probabilities.

She looks at the other unknown outcomes. She feels that if she works hard she has a good chance of success at college, probably 70%, leaving a 30% chance of failure. She adds these figures to the decision tree. University will be harder, but she still thinks she has a 60% chance of success, so a 40% chance of failure.

Copy and complete Figure 4.4 on p. 72 with the information given above.

Although this is more helpful, it is quite difficult to decide between 'a 10% chance of £20,000' and a 'a 90% chance of £6,000'. Anna needs straightforward figures to make a comparison.

She multiplies the £20,000 by its probability (10%), giving £2,000. This does not mean that she expects actually to earn £2,000. Rather, £2,000 is a convenient way of saying '£20,000 with a 10% chance of getting it'.

Figure 4.4

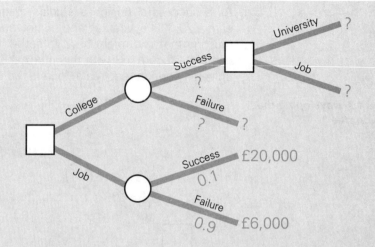

She does the same for £6,000 with a 90% chance of getting it, giving £5,400.

She can now work out what she would expect if she decides to get a job at 16, by adding together the £2,000 and £5,400 to give £7,400. Again she does not expect to be paid £7,400 – it is just a convenient way of summing up '£20,000, but with only a 10% chance of getting it and £6,000 with a 90% chance of getting it'. This figure of £7,400 is known as the **expected value**. She writes it at the unknown outcome point.

Copy and complete Figure 4.5 with the information given above. There should be an expected value at each node.

Figure 4.5

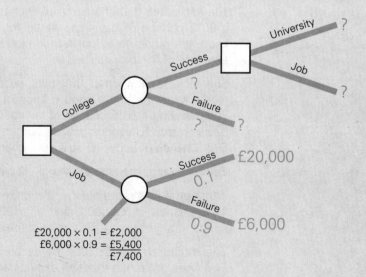

She now has a completed decision tree.

Making the decision

Anna starts at the very beginning of her decision tree. She has to make a decision now, on whether to go to college or get a job.

The expected value of getting a job is £7,400. Once the probabilities are included, the decision tree reveals the even more financially attractive option: that of going to college and thence to university.

Clearly if she decides on salary levels alone, she will opt for going to college, but not all decisions are made on the basis of money. What other factors might influence Anna in her decision and how might she take them into account?

Anna's view

'The decision tree was useful. Once I had drawn it, I realised that there were other possibilities – like getting a job with day release – which I hadn't even thought about. Also, it showed up exactly what information I needed to make a decision. I had to quantify it – for the first time, I really understood that I had very little chance of making a *fast buck* if I left school and got a job straight away. It also meant that I could tell my parents now that I wanted to go to university – that will give them a couple of years to save up!'

Within the context of a business, decision trees provide a focus for discussion as well as encouraging a logical and quantitative approach. In addition a decision tree not only specifies the expected values but it also weights these values by the probability of their actually occurring.

Against this, the most obvious drawback is that the figures are speculative. By putting quite specific values at each node there is a danger of giving them too much credibility. One answer to this is to gather as much information as possible so that the figures are as right as they possibly can be. The problem then is the cost of gathering that information, which might exceed any benefit gained from the exercise. It may also be necessary to produce two versions or more, showing optimistic, pessimistic, and most likely scenarios. Nevertheless the value of decision trees is clear, as long as the information is treated with the caution which all predictions containing numerate data should attract.

Open Question

Might there be some situations, or types of organisation, where decision trees are more useful than they are in others?

3 Investment appraisal

Opportunity cost

Capital investment is one of the most important areas for decision making in business. A business will have only a limited amount of capital available at any one time and there will be a range of possible alternatives on which to spend it. The business has to make a decision about which project to undertake and the managers will need to look at the costs of each alternative and the possible revenues.

Clearly, a company which invests in buildings or machinery must get it right, because such a decision commits it to a course of action for many years into the future. If the company had to reverse it, it could lose a great deal of money. Investment decisions are often strategic, moving the company along its strategic route, and any misjudgement could jeopardise the success of its long term planning.

Decisions about an investment are based on predictions concerning the future. These are both quantitative – about such things as interest rates and costs – and qualitative – about how well a product will perform against its competitors and about how consumer tastes will change.

Several techniques have been developed to help businesses to make investment decisions. One of the most straightforward ways of deciding between projects is to see which gives the greatest average rate of return on your investment.

Average rate of return

A firm has a choice between two projects:

Project A needs £3,000 investment. In the first year, it will make £2,500; in the second year, £4,000 and in the third year, £4,000.

Project B needs £6,000 investment. In the first year, it will make £3,500; in the second year, £4,000 and in the third year, £4,500.

This is set out more clearly as a table in Figure 4.6.

Figure 4.6 Average rate of return on two projects

		Project A (£)	Project B (£)
Investment (now)	Year 0	–3,000	–6,000
Cash inflows	Year 1	+2,500	+3,500
(End of year)	Year 2	+4,000	+4,000
	Year 3	+4,000	+4,500
Total cash inflows		+10,500	+12,000
Total net profit (Cash inflows less initial investment)		+7,500	+6,000
Average annual profit (Total net profit/no of years)		+2,500	+2,000

Average rate of return

Average rate of return (Average annual profit/Initial investment × 100)

$$\frac{2,500}{3,000} \times 100 \qquad \frac{2,000}{6,000} \times 100$$

$$= 83\% \qquad = 33\%$$

The percentage figures represent the percentage of the initial investment which is returned *on average* each year of the project.

If you were choosing between Project A and Project B on financial grounds alone, you would choose Project A because, on average, you get a higher return on your investment in each year of the project.

There is a problem with Average Rate of Return as a method of investment appraisal. Suppose you had to choose between Projects C and D using ARR – see Figure 4.7.

Figure 4.7 ARR and cash flow over time

		Project C (£)	Project D (£)
Investment	Year 0	10,000	10,000
Cash Inflows	Year 1	6,000	2,000
	Year 2	5,000	5,000
	Year 3	2,000	6,000
Total cash inflows		13,000	13,000
Total net profit		3,000	3,000
Average annual profit		1,000	1,000
Average rate of return		$\frac{1,000}{10,000} \times 100$	$\frac{1,000}{10,000} \times 100$
		= 10%	= 10%

The ARR of each project is the same, but there is a very good reason for preferring Project C.

If you chose Project C, you would get your money back much more quickly than if you chose Project D. The high cash inflows for Project C are in years 1 and 2; the high cash inflows for Project D are in years 2 and 3. The quicker you get your money back, the sooner you can reinvest it in new projects and make even more money.

The problem with ARR as a method of investment appraisal is that it hides the timing of the cash flows. As far as ARR is concerned, £6,000 in three years time is as good as £6,000 now.

A business has two possible investment projects – Project A and Project B – and is going to make its decision by comparing the average rate of return of each project.

The capital outlays and net returns for each project are:

		Project A	Project B
Capital outlay		£50,000	£180,000
Return:	Year 1	£12,000	£75,000
	Year 2	£12,000	£30,000
	Year 3	£12,000	£30,000
	Year 4	£12,000	£30,000
	Year 5	£12,000	£30,000

On the basis of ARR only, make a recommendation about which project the business should select.

What criteria, other than ARR, might you take into consideration when making your decision?

Discounted cash flows, present value and net present value

The previous Enquiry looked at Kristiana Cosmetics and its decision to move from making small quantities of specialist toothpaste, distributed through health food stores, to being a larger producer and distributing through high street shops. In order to achieve this objective the company is planning to invest money in new equipment and so it needs to apply *investment appraisal* methods to decide on which is best.

Kristiana Cosmetics (part 1)

As part of its five-year plan, Kristiana was considering investing £250,000 in production-line equipment. The marketing director, Dan Turner, was keen to go ahead.

'I know it's a great deal of money, but if we can't increase production, we will never get a high enough profile in the market. We need to get Kristiana into high street chemists and, at current production levels, they wouldn't even look at us.'

Lara Bowden, the finance director, was more cautious.

'It's a quarter of a million. What worries me is that we will buy this machinery, get ourselves into a high street store and then one of the big manufacturers will jump on to the bandwagon and undercut us. Bang goes our market and we've got £250,000 tied up in machinery. I think we should stick to the health food shops as an outlet – at least until we know what the competition is going to do.'

But Dan was determined.

'I've got market research which proves that we can sell enough to generate an extra £100,000 cash each year. The machine has a lifespan of five years, so we've got a surplus of £250,000. We get our place in the high street and £250,000 into the bargain.'

He passed the following figures round the table:

Year	Earnings
1	£100,000
2	£100,000
3	£100,000
4	£100,000
5	£100,000

'Hang on!' said Lara. 'You're forgetting that £100,000 next year is worth less than £100,000 today and in five years time, it will be worth even less. We need to look at those cash-in figures of yours in terms of what they are really worth. Interest rates are 10%. That means that money not invested anywhere is effectively going down in value by 10% a year.'

Being a resourceful person, Lara always carried her discounted cash flow tables around with her. These tables tell her what £1 will be worth in the future, at different rates of interest.

Future years	At 10% £1 today is worth
1	£0.909
2	£0.826
3	£0.751
4	£0.683
5	£0.621

She did a quick calculation on a sheet of paper and then passed it to Dan.

£100,000 in 1 year's time is worth $100,000 \times 0.909 = £90,900$

£100,000 in 2 years' time is worth $100,000 \times 0.826 = £82,600$

£100,000 in 3 years' time is worth $100,000 \times 0.751 = £75,100$

£100,000 in 4 years' time is worth $100,000 \times 0.683 = £68,300$

£100,000 in 5 years' time is worth $100,000 \times 0.621 = £62,100$

'Add those cash flows up and you get £379,000. That's a lot different from £500,000!'

Asset and liabilities

Companies buy machinery, premises, tools and equipment. These are the assets of the business, which are used to make a profit. The most successful and profitable companies make the most efficient use of their assets, so decisions about which assets should be acquired and how much money should be invested are vitally important.

Kristiana Cosmetics had to make a decision about whether to invest £250,000 in machinery. The management team had several different issues to bear in mind when making their decision.

ROCE

RONA

The £250,000 came from retained profits. This was the maximum amount available for investment, so only one project could be undertaken. If the project were to be unsuccessful, the business will not just have lost the £250,000, it will also have lost the amount of money it could have generated had the £250,000 been successfully invested. This is the opportunity cost of the £250,000. This is why, as Lara showed, money in the future is not worth as much as money today.

Inflation

An investment decision today will be made on the basis of the amount of money you expect to make from that investment in the future. Inflation means that prices are rising – you might need £1 to buy a box of chocolate today, but £1.10 in a year's time. The spending power of each pound falls by an amount which depends on the rate of inflation; more pounds will be needed for each to have the same value.

Most investments are intended to generate money over a period of time – usually several years, so the first step is to predict the amount of money which the investment should generate each year (the cash inflow). This cash inflow each year is then discounted, to take account of the timing of the cash flow and the loss of interest on the funds involved in the investment. The discounted cash flows are then added up, to provide the **present value**, which reflects the fact that pounds in future cash flows are worth less than pounds in cash flows today. Kristiana's present value amounted to £379,000.

Once the present value has been calculated, the initial investment is subtracted from it, giving the **net present value** (NPV). The NPV of an investment is its value, in today's pounds, less the initial capital outlay, which in Kristiana's case is £129,000.

Kristiana's decision cannot be made on the grounds of cash flows alone. It depends as much on the company's beliefs about its competitors as on the DCF calculations. It might calculate the discounted cash flows perfectly and *prove* that the investment is worthwhile, but if a large manufacturer decides to move into Kristiana's market, undercut it and force it out of business, its DCF calculations will turn out to be rather different from reality. Financial decisions cannot be divorced from the wider social and ethical environment in which a business has to operate.

At Kristiana, Dan estimated that if he bought the machine, it would produce £100,000 cash a year, over five years. He added these cash flows up and stated that the £250,000 invested would produce £500,000 cash.

Lara showed that this was not so. She accepted that the cash flow each year would be £100,000, but discounted it to take account of the fact that £100,000 in future years would be worth less than £100,000 now. She added up the cash flows, which came to £379,000 less the initial investment of £250,000, leaving £129,000. This is the net present value of the investment – how much the investment is really worth.

Kristiana Cosmetics (part 2)

Before a decision had been made on whether to invest in the machine, Lara looked at the first draft of the year-end figures.

'We've got £80,000 left in the capital expenditure budget,' she said to Dan. 'I'll draft a memo, inviting proposals for the investment of this sum. I'll get it out to the departmental managers by the end of the week and give them a fortnight to put together their bids.'

Within two days of the memo being sent, the distribution department replied. Steve Jackson, the departmental manager, had been talking about replacing the four 10-year-old lorries for some time. The problem was that there had never been enough money. The trucks were a tribute to the mechanics who maintained them, and so they were still reliable, but they were well past their prime.

Steve asked for four new lorries, at a cost of £20,000 each. They should last five years, after which time they could each be sold for £5,000.

Lara called Steve into her office.

'I know the trucks are old, but they're still reliable. How can I sell the idea of buying new ones to the board?'

'Well,' replied Steve, 'I've looked at the new vehicles and they should be able to carry at least 50% more than the current ones. That means that we can make fewer delivery journeys. Also, the garage bills should be far less – with fewer breakdowns and cheaper servicing. I have estimated that we should be able to save £5,000 per vehicle per year. And if we do decide to go ahead with the new production line equipment, we will need the extra delivery capacity.'

A week later, Lara got another bid – this time from the marketing department.

MEMORANDUM

To: Lara Bowden
From: Dan Turner
Date: 7 October 1994

MARKETING SUPPORT FOR INCREASED SALES

The £100,000 extra profit a year which results from the new production line equipment will require an increase in sales volume of over 50%.

At present, the marketing department deals with customer support — all the queries and complaints come through to us and we deal with them.

The marketing department will not be able to cope with a possible increase of over 50% in customer service activities, so I suggest that a customer liaison manager be appointed to deal with this.

There will be initial costs of £5,000 — for office furniture and a PC and, after that, I think a salary at a level of about £18,000 a year plus £2,000 a year contribution to administrative overheads.

If we can't afford a customer liaison manager, we won't be able to achieve the extra £100,000 profit!

I am attaching calculations showing the costs and revenues associated with my bid:

INVESTMENT APPRAISAL FIGURES FOR THE NEW MACHINE
PLUS MARKETING SUPPORT

1 **NEW MACHINE** — assuming a cost of £250,000 and £100,000 addition to profit per year over the next five years.

```
£100,000 in 1 year's time is worth 100,000 x 0.909 = £ 90,900
£100,000 in 2 years' time is worth 100,000 x 0.826 = £ 82,600
£100,000 in 3 years' time is worth 100,000 x 0.751 = £ 75,100
£100,000 in 4 years' time is worth 100,000 x 0.683 = £ 68,300
£100,000 in 5 years' time is worth 100,000 x 0.621 = £ 62,100
                                                       £379,000
```

Present value of investment = £379,000

```
2 MARKETING SUPPORT — Assuming an initial cost of £5,000 and then
yearly additional costs of £20,000.
         Costs      Present value
Year 0   £ 5,000    £ 5,000
Year 1   £20,000    £18,180
Year 2   £20,000    £16,520
Year 3   £20,000    £15,020
Year 4   £20,000    £13,660
Year 5   £20,000    £12,420
                    £80,800

So, the new machinery plus the necessary Marketing Support will give us
£379,000 — £80,800 = £298,200
```

Lara looked at the documents. With the additional information which resulted from her memo, she would have to re-work all the figures, putting them into a format which would make the data clear. The board would need all the information about the impact of the new machinery before they could make a decision. But, first, she would have to sort out Dan's figures – they were a shambles.

Using evidence from Kristiana 1 and 2, critically examine Steve and Dan's arguments. What is right and what is wrong with what they say?

Draft Lara's report to the board, setting out the advantages and disadvantages of each project.

On the quantitative evidence alone, which project would you recommend? On the quantitative and qualitative evidence, which project would you recommend?

Internal rate of return

The internal rate of return is another way of using DCF calculations to help estimate the value of future work.

Greening scrap

'We refurbish production-line equipment. When large factories replace their production lines, we buy up the equipment, repair and service it and then sell it on to smaller businesses. Sometimes we sell a complete line; at other times, we sell individual machines. It's funny how things change. We used to be very downmarket – looked on as little better than scrap merchants! Of course, now we're "into recycling" and that's all very green.

'Anyway, in 1985, we were asked to bid for a five-year maintenance contract for a local factory. I was looking to diversify and it seemed sensible to move from repairing our own machinery to repairing other people's. We really wanted the job, to establish ourselves in the maintenance market. I

spent a lot of time putting the tender together. I reckoned that we would need tools and equipment, which would cost about £7,500. I was happy to take the job on a "no profit" basis, simply to get it, but the business could not afford a loss.

'I reckoned that, if I put in a tender for the contract at £2,000 a year, we would break even. I estimated interest rates averaging 10% over the duration of the project and discounted the cash flows, giving a present value of £7,580. That covered our costs and I was happy.

'The problem was that interest rates averaged 15% over the contract. I redid the sums and we ended up with a present value of £6,706. Less the initial investment, we ended up £794 in the red.' – Tony Stewart

Tony's problem was that he did not take into account possible future changes in interest rates, which would affect the 'correct' rate at which to discount future cash flows. At a discount rate of 10%, the NPV of the maintenance contract was £7,580 – £7,500 = £80. This means that, at a discount rate of just above 10%, the NPV of the project will be zero. At a discount rate significantly above 10%, the NPV of the project would be negative. At a discount rate significantly below 10%, the NPV of the project will be positive. Figure 4.8 shows the NPV calculations for discount rates of 5%, 10% and 15%.

Figure 4.8 DCF calculations

Tender price for a project yielding £2,000 per year for five years at discount rates of 5%, 10%, 15%.

	Cash inflow	Discount rate	Present value
At 5%	2,000	0.952	1,904
	2,000	0.906	1,812
	2,000	0.863	1,726
	2,000	0.822	1,644
	2,000	0.784	1,568
			8,654
At 10%	2,000	0.909	1,818
	2,000	0.826	1,652
	2,000	0.751	1,502
	2,000	0.683	1,366
	2,000	0.621	1,242
			7,580
At 15%	2,000	0.870	1,740
	2,000	0.756	1,512
	2,000	0.658	1,316
	2,000	0.572	1,144
	2,000	0.497	994
			6,706

NPV at   5%   = £8,654 – £7,500 = £1,154
          10%   = £7,580 – £7,500 = £80
          15%   = £6,706 – £7,500 = –£794

When Kristiana was considering its new production line, Lara discounted the figures at a rate of 10%. This yielded a value of £379,000 instead of £500,000.

If she had discounted her cash flows at 20%, the total cash inflows would have been worth £312,000. So as the rate at which you discount the cash flow increases, the net present value of the investment decreases.

The **internal rate of return (IRR)** of the project is the discount rate at which the NPV is zero. In Tony's case, it is just above 10%.

Plotting this information on a graph makes it clearer. The first point to plot is where the discount rate is zero. That would mean that the £10,000 (£2000 per year) would also be £10,000 in today's money, and the net present value would be £10,000 – £7,500 = £2,500. From the calculations in Figure 4.8 the net present value figures at discount rates of 5, 10 and 15% can be plotted, as shown in Figure 4.9.

Figure 4.9 Net present value

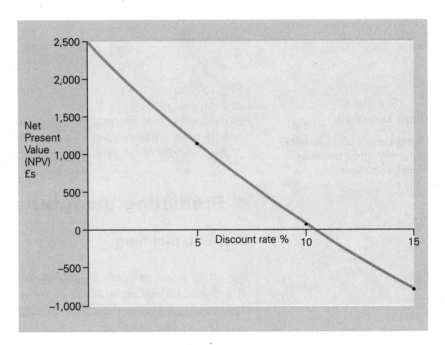

Relatively small changes in interest rates up or down from the estimated 10% have a considerable effect on the profitability of this project.

Tony Stewart continues: 'I suppose that, if I had done the IRR graph, it would have helped me. I could have seen how risky my position was. There was nothing that I could have done about my estimate of interest rates – I was working on the best information I had. The problem was that I did not take on board how risky my position was – how much I would be affected by relatively small changes in interest rates.

With hindsight, I think I would have set the yearly contract sum slightly higher. I think I would have gone for a more positive NPV, to reduce the risk of a loss at the end of the day. It was simply too risky to plan a project on the basis of "just breaking even" when changes in interest rates could have such a devastating effect.'

How might Tony have covered himself from the possibility of changing interest rates?

Using the internal rate of return technique to make an investment decision

The financial director of a company has received a request for £2,000 to be invested in Project A. He has the following information:

Initial investment £2,000
Cash inflows

	Year 1	£500
	Year 2	£550
	Year 3	£600
	Year 4	£650
	Year 5	£700

Should he allow the project to go ahead:
a) if interest rates were 12%;
b) if interest rates were 12%, but inflation had started to rise;
c) if he were offered a five year fixed-rate bank loan at 14%;
d) if he were offered a five year fixed-rate bank loan at 10%?

Open Question

How does inflation impact generally upon business decision making?

4 Predicting the future

Scenario planning

Instead of using past data to predict the future, a new development in planning is to explore a range of scenarios, challenging current ideas. This approach liberates thinking and allows a number of alternatives to be given serious attention.

Throw Away Lines

Throw Away Lines is a refuse collection company. It is a public limited company, operating in a large city in the North. A year ago, Throw Away Lines won the tender to take over refuse collection from the local authority team and the business looks set to grow.

The managing director of the company is working on the 10-year development plan. At the moment, the business is profitable and the contract with the local authority looks secure. She is conscious that the success of the business is largely due to government policies and competitive tendering – it has benefited from radical changes in local authority services. She is anxious to make sure that the business remains profitable, even if there are changes in government policy, and in the social and economic climate.

She calls her management team together and they brainstorm ideas about what the future may hold. They come up with five alternative future scenarios, then split into groups to spell out in more detail what each will be like.

Scenario 1 – Rosy future

No political change. Economy improves gradually and consumer confidence increases. We consolidate our position, gaining a good reputation for value for money. Gradual increase in the number of authorities offering refuse collection to tender. Previous experience puts us in a strong position to win tenders and expand in a controlled way. Environmental legislation provides incentives for recycling, but no compulsion. Established companies take control of the market, setting prices and levels of service.

Scenario 2 – Council goes green

Public opinion favours 'green' policies – regardless of political party. Local authority reasserts control over refuse collection, even though lack of public money means that services remain in the private sector. Stringent regulations about standards and quality. Tenderers for refuse collection must offer recycling services; there are some local authority grants for recycling centres, where refuse can be 'dumped' only if sorted. Local authority 'dumps' are converted to recycling centres, where refuse can be 'dumped' only if sorted for recycling. Householders are required to pre-sort rubbish, complicating refuse collection.

Scenario 3 – Most likely

Reasonable political stability. More authorities offering refuse collection to tender, but the main criterion is price, so we have to trim profit margins/cut costs. Smaller operators and foreign companies move into the market, competing on price either by having lower overheads or penetration pricing. Increasing public awareness of 'green' issues and demand for recycling (although there is a general unwillingness either to pay a premium or to sort refuse) prompts local authority to demand additional services at little/no extra cost.

Scenario 4 – Free market

The structure of local authorities changes – they become 'enabling authorities', whose only function is to issue tenders. There is no local authority to control local services and the responsibility for ensuring standards is unclear. Increasing pressure to lower local taxes means that tenders are issued mainly on price. The market in the city fragments and new entrants win tenders for small, easy to work areas on price alone, although they provide a poor level of service and there are frequent complaints. Local authority tied to tenderers for three years, which means that it is difficult to put pressure on them to improve standards in the short term. Pressure on costs means that, in the short term, there are few recycling facilities. In the longer term, recycling centres are introduced (national/European Parliament legislation?) and the public are encouraged to take their own refuse to be recycled.

Scenario 5 – Worst case

Political instability – resulting in uncertainty about the future of tendering for services. Possibility of either reverting to local authority operatives or strict controls on pricing/conditions for private operators. Smaller operators enter the market, increasing price competition and, in the short term, winning tenders. We cannot risk undercutting them to drive them out of the market, because we do not know whether we will be in the market long enough to recoup our costs.

These are not all the possible scenarios – just the ones which the management team considers to be the most likely. They are credible not only because they are based on current trends, but also because they have been written by a management team which has sound, broad knowledge of the area.

The Throw Away Lines management team used scenario planning as a way of predicting the future. Of course, no one knows for certain what will happen, but we can be fairly sure about some things: for instance, whichever party is elected in the next General Election, it is unlikely that there will be a massive programme of nationalisation. Other things are not so clear: there have been rapid developments in information technology over the last few years and it is difficult to imagine what sorts of IT systems could be in place in 20 years' time. Sometimes things happen which simply cannot be predicted in advance, such as the Gulf War and the civil war in Bosnia. Even though it cannot know what the future will be like, an organisation has to make decisions now, in the hope that the choices which it makes will be the right ones for the future.

What is a scenario?

A *scenario* is a description of a state of affairs. For Throw Away Lines, the state of affairs in question is 'What will it be like in the year ...?' Not everything about the year in a scenario has to be described, just those aspects which are of interest to the company. Throw Away Lines is concerned about government policies and public attitudes to waste management. A petrol company might write scenarios which include predictions about developments in automotive technology, oil prices and environmental legislation. A charity might write scenarios about government spending, people's disposable incomes and changes in public attitudes to certain causes.

Scenario planning is a powerful tool for decision making. An organisation can write a set of scenarios, setting out different possibilities for how things might be. Each should be significantly different from the others and the series should cover the broad range of possibilities about the future. Throw Away Lines was covering all its options by writing a range of scenarios that included 'best possible', 'worst possible' and 'most likely' cases.

These scenarios do not have to be very detailed. They simply provide an outline of the future. If the predictions are too detailed, then they are more likely to be wrong. Working with incorrect scenarios is more likely to yield a wrong decision now. Firms need scenarios which are broad enough to enable them to plan for as many outcomes as possible.

What should go into a scenario?

Scenario planning is really only an interesting way of looking at constraints on decision making. A set of scenarios indicates a vision of the future and describes the circumstances which will constrain any decisions made by an organisation's management team.

SWOT analysis

Scenarios must include predictions about the environment in which a business will be operating. Threats and opportunities should be noted.

> You are the long-term planning manager of a large chain of fast-food restaurants. Write three alternative future scenarios for the environment in which the fast-food business will have to operate in the next ten years.

There are a number of factors which together form the 'environment' in which a business operates.

The *economic* environment: a building company might welcome rising house prices, because this encourages people to buy houses as soon as they can, in the expectation that prices will continue to rise in the future. The business will want to know what fiscal policies it can expect – will taxes be high or low? Will the government favour direct taxes or indirect? Will certain items (such as fuel or alcohol) be targeted? It will want to know about monetary policy – if the firm is highly geared, rises in interest rates can push costs up sharply.

Gearing

Fiscal and monetary policy

The *political* environment: it is clearly important to know which political party is likely to be in power and what their policies will be. It is not safe to assume that every business favours a Conservative government. Many businesses provide goods and services to the public sector; a government which forces public sector cuts might be very unpopular with them.

The *technological* environment: improvements in technology can be an opportunity if a company can benefit from them, but a threat if competitors are more successful at exploiting them. The competition between different video recorders is a good example of this, with the Betamax system of Philips and Sony, two major innovators, losing out to the rival VHS system.

The *social* environment: this can change rapidly. The things that worry people have changed: a few years ago, environmentally friendly washing powder was only found in health food shops. Now, it is available in most supermarkets.

There are changes in *demography*: people are living longer and companies are providing services to the relatively wealthy 'third agers' – people who have retired in their late 50s and have time, health and money to spend on leisure.

Moving averages

Scenario planning uses qualitative information to make predictions about the future. Sometimes quantitative information about the past is available and this can be used to make predictions. Moving averages can be used for this. They smooth out information so that extreme data are removed and the underlying trend is revealed. This trend line can be extended into the future, to give a predicted trend. Extending it in this way is called **extrapolating**.

Moving averages

Of course, the trend figure is not the same as the actual figures, which will be above or below the trend. For instance, if sales were seasonal and the fourth quarter had peak sales, that figure would be above the trend. The second quarter, with the lowest figures, would be below it. The difference between the actual figure and the trend figure is known as the *seasonal variation*.

Moving averages have to be treated with caution, as do all predictions about the future. The external factors outlined above could suddenly cause past events to be irrelevant or unreliable, or a larger trend could superimpose itself on the existing one. In the end the crucial point is that just because something always happened in the past it does not mean that it will continue to happen in the future!

5 New methods of decision making

The unreliability of past data as a way of predicting the future has led some management thinkers to consider alternative ways forward. It is difficult, and sometimes misleading to put figures on choices. It is usually far easier and more accurate to put choices in an order. Take the case of Deena Patel.

Choosing a career

Deena Patel is 18 years of age, and talented. She is expected to gain four excellent A level grades. She is extrovert, caring and enjoys working with people. Her economics and business teacher has asked her to make a detailed appraisal of the possible alternative careers of chairperson of an oil company or a nurse. Deena's reply was as follows:

'Well, if I go for chairperson, I will make £15 million over the next 30 years; as a nurse, I would be lucky to make £500,000. Of course, there is the satisfaction that I would gain from

being a nurse – let's put a figure of £5 million on that and perhaps £3 million of satisfaction for being the chairperson. I think I'll gather more information on the amount of time that I will have left to spend with my family for each option. Now, if I reckon that each hour of family time is worth £10.00 ....'

At the end of the exercise Deena felt more confused than before, and certainly her choice of career had not been helped. She felt that somehow her instincts had been denied.

Deena's problem was that it is incredibly difficult to put a price on the costs and benefits of any course of action. Sometimes you simply 'know' that one thing is much better or much worse than another. You do not need to be able to give a precise figure of how much better or worse, and the time and effort needed if you tried to do this would far outweigh the benefits of going through a systematic decision making process. There may also be a clear ethical reason for choosing, or not choosing particular routes.

Instead of trying to make her decision on quantifiable evidence, it would have been far easier and just as useful for Deena to have said, 'If I were a nurse, I would be 10 times more satisfied than if I were a company chairperson.' She might even plot it on a satisfaction scale:

Figure 4.10 A satisfaction scale

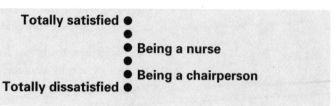

A satisfaction scale is one kind of **preference scale**. A preference scale is used when you have a range of possible courses of action. Some are a lot better and some a lot worse than others. Instead of trying to quantify each, you plot them, putting the worst course of action at one end and the best at the other. Then you range the others across the scale. If there is little to choose between two options, you put them close together.

Saturday night – boring!

It's Saturday night and Sam is going out with a group of friends. There is a range of possible activities and no one can agree what to do: there is the cinema, bowling, the theatre, swimming, badminton or watching a video.

Sam hates swimming and loves the cinema, so he plots them on his preference scale. A video comes a close second to the cinema. He is indifferent to badminton and bowling – perhaps bowling is slightly better. Going to the theatre would be better than sport.

Sam's preference scale is:

LOVE ....HATE
Cinema Video   Theatre   Bowling Badminton   Swimming

Recently, the idea of using preference scales has been applied to business decision making. Instead of using actual or estimated cost and benefit figures, managers talk about one course of action being preferable to another and about how much more or less preferable it is.

Preference scales are part of a new approach to decision making which, although it is based on more traditional and systematic methods, is far more intuitive and flexible.

Options and criteria

When weighing up a course of action, some things will be important and others less so. For example, when you are looking for a job, one of the most important things will be the prospects for promotion and progression. You may also think that salary or benefits are very important, whilst, if you have a car or good public transport, the distance to work from home may not be very important. On the other hand, for a disabled person, the ease of the journey to work may be the most important criterion when deciding whether or not to take a job. Some people choose jobs on the basis of the standard of living they will be able to achieve; others are more concerned with the quality of their working life.

Decisions are made by looking both at the options – the alternative courses of action available – and at the criteria – the factors by which you judge the options.

Buying a fleet of company cars

Simon Beckett is the fleet car manager for a large company. Every two years, he has to choose the make of car which the sales representatives will be given.

a) Setting out the options

Simon begins by setting out the options. There are three possibilities: car A at £18,000, car B at £13,200 and car C at £12,000.

b) Deciding on the criteria

Simon needs to choose between the cars, so he needs criteria for making that choice. The obvious criteria are *cost* and *benefit*.

The cost criterion is quite simple – it is the price of the car. The benefit criteria are more difficult, because there are lots of possible benefits – the engine size, the trim, and so on, but there is little between the cars on these criteria. Simon has found that the sales representatives are very conscious of the status of the vehicle they drive – their most important benefit criterion is the *brand*, so Simon uses this.

c) Quantifying the options

Cost is an easily quantifiable criterion. The most preferred car on the cost criterion alone will be the cheapest one.

The most preferred option is given a score of 100 – so car C, as the cheapest, scores 100 on price. The least preferred is given a score of 0 – so car A, the dearest, gets 0.

The difference in price between car A and car C

is £6,000. Car B costs £1,200 more than car C. This is 20% of the difference between car A and car B. Car B is therefore 20% worse than car C on price, so scores 80 on the preference scale.

The figures for cost are relatively easy to calculate and plot on the preference scale as shown in figure 4.11, so it is worth doing the sums! It would be almost impossible to do similar calculations for brand, so this has to be done intuitively.

Figure 4.11 A preference scale

The most preferred brand for the sales representatives is car A, so it scores 100. Car C is the least preferred, so scores zero and the car B is almost as good as car A, so it scores 80. This approach is sometimes called **intuitive decision making**. This is because the score given to a particular option, in this case on the brand criterion, must be decided intuitively, since it cannot be quantified in any other way.

d) Showing what is important

Some criteria for decision making are more important than others – they are therefore given more weight.

Although Simon likes to keep his sales representatives happy, he is answerable to a finance director. The cost of the cars is far more important than the brand. In fact, his decision will be 90% based on cost and only 10% based on brand. To show this, he weights the cost by 0.9 and the benefit by 0.1.

e) Making the information easier to understand

These figures can be put on a spreadsheet as in Figure 4.12. This shows the score given to each car on the basis of cost and the weight given to cost as a decision making criterion. In the third column we have score × weight, or the weighted score. All this information is on the cost side of the spreadsheet.

Figure 4.12 Weighting the criteria

	Cost			Benefit		
	score	weight	weighted score	score	weight	weighted score
Car A	0	0.9	0	100	0.1	10
Car B	80	0.9	72	80	0.1	8
Car C	100	0.9	90	0	0.1	0

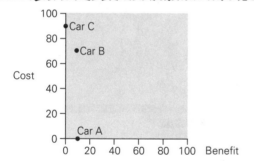

On the benefit side, the same procedure is followed. When the spreadsheet is complete, it can all be transferred to a graph. Plotting the benefit scores on the horizontal and the cost scores on the vertical, each car can be positioned on the graph. The best buy, taking both the weighted criteria into consideration, will be the one which is furthest from the origin.

The graph is really only a way of showing what is intuitively obvious. If you are concerned primarily about the price and the brand is much less important, buy car C.

f) Manipulating the data

Simon can use his computer to do 'What if ...' calculations. If the finance director gave him more money and the brand name became equally important to the price, what would the decision be? He changes the weights to 0.5 for each, as shown in Figure 4.13.

Figure 4.13 Different weights

	Cost			Benefit		
	score	weight	weighted score	score	weight	weighted score
Car A	0	0.5	0	100	0.5	50
Car B	80	0.5	40	80	0.5	40
Car C	100	0.5	50	0	0.5	0

What is Simon's decision now?

Business criteria

Businesses have different concerns when decision making and Figure 4.14 on page 91 is the result of research into the priority concerns of businesses.

This information is very interesting to analyse, especially given the differences which are apparent between large and small scale operations. It is interesting to note, however, how important defining a five-year strategy is, and how relatively unimportant defining a strategy beyond that is. That is not unreasonable perhaps, given a political, social and economic climate which tends at times to fall into such a cycle. It will be the case, of course, that many of the firms surveyed for this information simply will not be in existence in five years' time. The key question is, would they have been if they had lifted their sights a shade beyond this immediate climate? Perhaps what is needed is a radical approach such as the one which has been imported from Japan in recent years.

It is to the wider horizon that we now turn for Enquiry 5.

Fig 4.14 Priority concerns

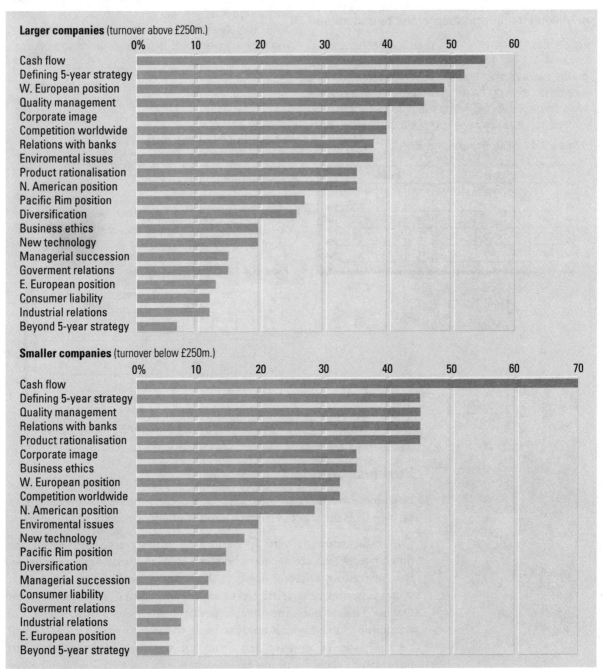

Source: *Independent on Sunday,* 25 July 1993

Enquiry 5: What are the constraints on decision making?

Scope

Business decisions depend on the availability of alternatives. Sometimes different courses of action are ruled out simply because they are impossible, impractical, or because they run counter to the company's ethical position. Such limitations can be imposed both from within and from outside the organisation and although it may be possible to influence them they can rarely, if ever, be controlled. Clearly, those constraints which are internal can be more easily changed by firms, and the Japanese have led the way in structuring their organisations to enable this to take place. As a result, many Japanese practices have found their way into European business, but the philosophy of importing Japanese ideas wholesale into a different context is increasingly the subject of controversy and debate.

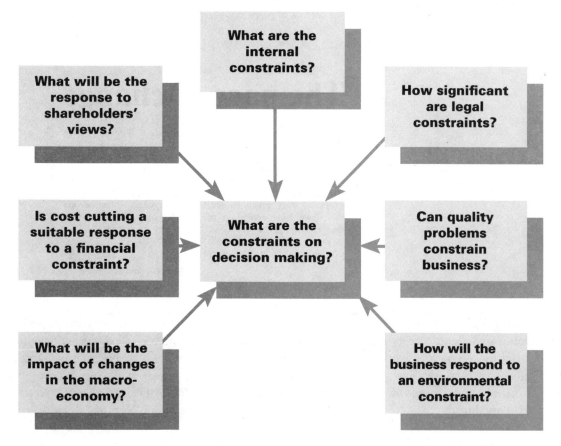

Opening evidence

'We make window frames – just the ordinary ones, for domestic use. Last year, we started to get complaints. Nothing awful, I suppose, but more than we have ever had before. They were mostly about the finish on the wood – it was rough and difficult to paint.

'I mentioned the problem at the next departmental meeting and said that I wanted to spend a bit of time working out how to solve these sorts of problems. The next thing I know, this chap arrives from head office, a "finance manager", with all sorts of graphs and diagrams. The one that worried me the most looked rather like this:

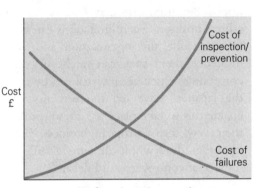

He told me that this graph *proved* that it was better to have up to five quality complaints a month than none at all! This finance manager told me that he had worked it out. The costs incurred by having five or less quality problems a week – things like reworking frames, replacing defective goods – was less than the costs of preventing those defects. By that, I suppose he means it's cheaper to put problems right when customers notice them than to get the goods checked before they leave the factory. Anyway, given that we had never had five complaints a month, he said that we couldn't afford better quality.' – Paul, works manager

The pace of change

JAPANESE management, which already has experience of the culture shock its methods created in the United States, is nevertheless puzzled by what it sees as the British refusal to adopt its work practices until they have been convinced of their efficacy. A completed and, in theory, defect-free car rolls off the production line every 60 seconds at Tsutsumi. What could be more persuasive?

For Kosuke Ikebuchi, director of the Tsutsumi plant, the Britons' strong point is that they are hardworking and diligent. 'Their weakness is that they are not willing to compromise unless they are convinced.'

Source: *Guardian*, 27 May 1992

'Competition for the sake of competition has dominated and everything was sacrificed, including wages, working hours, profits, subcontractors, dealers, the lives of Japanese workers and employment opportunities of workers abroad.

Even if one beats competition in such a manner, can it really be called fair competition? When competition itself becomes an end and people can begin to compete at all costs, it becomes a monster that can destroy life, society and even the economy.' – Professor Haruo Shimada, Keio University

'... Let me tell you about two meetings I sat in on. Both were with companies that were having problems with quality control. One company was professionally managed. Their approach to the problem was to analyse everything. How many doors, say, were falling off? What percentage of doors were falling off? How much would it cost to stick 'em back on? What were the chances of getting sued? How much advertising would it take to counteract the bad publicity? Not once did they actually talk about the doors, the hinges or why the hell they were falling off. They weren't interested in solving the problem, they just wanted to manage the mess. The other meeting was at Coleman Stove ... They were having a problem with some boilers that were cracking. So picture it – the Executive Committee assembles, there's the usual small talk ... Then the service department comes in with the reports, the clipboards, the yellow pencils, and everybody hunkers down for a serious discussion. Well, you know how long that meeting lasted? About thirty seconds: Old Man Coleman sits bolt upright in his chair and bellows out: "You mean we've got goods out there that aren't working? Get 'em back. Replace 'em and find out why, goddammit." And that was the end of the meeting. There was no financial analysis. There was no legal analysis. There was no customer-relations analysis. There was no goddam analysis. The issue was the integrity of the product – which meant there was no issue at all. We stand by it, and that's that.'

Source: Conrad Jones of Booz Allen & Hamilton, in *The Big Time*, quoted in Tom Peters, *Thriving on Chaos*, Pan Books, 1987

Some argue that businesses have a responsibility to act ethically. Those who hold this view stress the fact that firms do not operate in isolation. They are a part of society and have an impact upon the lives of those communities in which they operate. As such they should act in a socially responsible manner and consider the possible effects of any decisions they make. This means that profit making should not be the only criterion used when making decisions. Other factors which firms might consider include the effect of their decisions upon the environment, jobs, the local community, consumers, competitors, suppliers and employees.

Source: Ian Chambers (ed.), *Business Studies*, Causeway Press, 1993

The impact of recovery

THE pace of economic recovery in the East Midlands has quickened, says the regional group of chambers of commerce.

The chambers concluded after canvassing 323 companies that 51% of them had improved domestic order books compared with 40% at the end of last year.

Although 34% of companies are expecting to recruit more labour over the next three months and 51% are expecting higher profitability, fewer than a third of companies were operating at full capacity. Cashflow is still a major worry.

Source: *Financial Times*, 26 April 1994

'I went for an interview for a teaching post. I arrived at the school and was shown into the headmaster's study. It was all very formal and I knew straight away that this was not the job for me.

As we were walking around the school, I said to the headmaster, "Could you tell me about your equal opportunities policy?"

"Madam," he replied. "We don't need an equal opportunities policy in this school. *I treat everyone exactly the same.*"

Needless to say, I didn't get the job!'

1 Constraints on decision making

As an individual you are constrained in your decision making. You see a pair of shoes which you would like, but you also want a new pair of jeans. You cannot afford both – you are constrained by your finances. You would like to go out but you have homework to do – you are constrained by time. Similarly businesses are constrained – they cannot do all that they would wish.

Opportunity cost

No business operates in a vacuum. It is influenced by the business around it, the society in which it operates and the people both within and outside it. These things determine what the business can do and how it can do it; they are constraints on the business – they can persuade a business to follow a certain course of action, or can dissuade it. In some cases looking at constraints on business activity can show up new and creative ways for the business to operate.

Internal constraints

Internal constraints are to do with what the business has decided that it wants to do, with the resources it has, operating within the kind of organisation that it is. These internal constraints are as follows:

- The objectives of the organisation – if the objective is to increase overall market share, the sales department might be constrained in its actions – perhaps it cannot achieve its own internal objective of reducing costs by withdrawing from less profitable segments of the market.
- Resources – no organisation has unlimited finance, materials or personnel; different interest groups in a company must compete for resources.
- Corporate culture – some kinds of behaviour are simply not acceptable in certain organisations. Some hierarchical organisations constrain very tightly the kinds of decisions which people at different levels may take.

Shareholders and decision making

In business, everyone makes decisions – from strategic ones made at board level to everyday decisions made on the shop floor.

Stakeholders

Employees who make decisions are responsible to their line manager, for instance, a production worker might be responsible to the production manager. Managers are responsible to the directors who represent the interests of the shareholders. Executive directors are the top managers in a company – they are involved in its running and they make decisions.

Non-executive directors are not involved in the running of the company. They are members of the board because they have particular experience which enables them to assist and advise. Because they are not directly involved in the day-to-day decision making process, they are often able to stand back and offer a balanced view.

Shareholders are the owners of the company and elect the board of directors. They seldom wish to have an influence on everyday decision making and, until recently, did not seem to have much interest in the operations of a business.

Lately, there have been changes. Shareholders have started to become more involved. The Washington-based United Shareholders Association (USA) was formed as a response to poor management in some public limited companies. It targets companies which it feels are under-performing.

In theory poor management should result in a take-over, or the firm going into liquidation. In practice many companies which are taken over by new management teams do not improve their performance. One inefficient management team is simply replaced by another.

If takeovers or threatened takeovers are not a check on inefficient management, then shareholders themselves will have to become actively involved. USA represents the owners of millions of shares, so companies have to take notice of what it says. It has successfully forced management changes in some of America's largest companies.

Ethical money urged to target offending firms

NEW Consumer, a charity, believes in shareholder action to change business. Ethically minded investors should consider buying shares in companies with dodgy products and poor working practices, and disinvesting from firms with cleaner track-records.

This apparently odd idea, contradicting everything that existing 'ethical' funds practise, is one of a number of suggestions made by Craig Mackenzie, a researcher with the New Consumer, a Newcastle-based charity, in its *Shareholder Action Handbook*, published this month.

Mr Mackenzie believes that investment in companies with poor ethical and social performance allows more opportunities for 'energetic shareholder action campaigns for reform'. He is sceptical of the effectiveness of traditional ethical investment.

'Negative screening encourages ethically motivated people to silently sell their share and move to a "clean" company, with little practical impact except a clearer conscience for the investor,' he said.

More generally, Mr Mackenzie wants to encourage greater participation by shareholders, not only in issues of social responsibility, in companies which (at least theoretically) they part-own. 'Shareholders are not expected to have any responsibilities. But if you read company law, the whole idea behind it is that shareholders must participate in running their companies.'

He maintains that shareholders also help to promote their own interests by taking a more active role. 'There are an awful lot of directors who are not pulling their weight or earning their salaries and wouldn't be there if there was a very vociferous shareholder lobby. Shareholder activism would serve to increase the economic efficiency of companies,' he said.

Mr Mackenzie also suggests that Britain still has some way to go to catch up with the level of

citizen shareholder activism in the United States. 'Last year, several hundred companies in the US faced socially motivated shareholder action campaigns,' he said.

Source: *Independent on Sunday*, 17 January 1993

Shareholders and short-termism

Businesses must satisfy their shareholders, who can express dissatisfaction by selling their shares. Some people argue that this gives British companies a very short-term attitude to decision making – maximising short-term profits and hence dividends, at the expense of long-term investment. In reply, these companies say that, unless they can show healthy annual profits to pay increasing dividends to their shareholders, those shareholders simply sell the shares.

The decisions which a company makes are constrained by the *response* of the shareholders. Some people have argued that the problem of short-termism in the British economy is structural – it is because shares in companies are held by investors who are not committed to that company.

For example, a business might want to invest heavily in new equipment and training for its staff. It needs to retain profits to do this, so it declares a lower than usual dividend. Everyone knows that the company's actions will be good in the long term. The future profitability of the company will be increased by investment now. The problem is that a small shareholder in the company can see that if he sells his shares in that company and invests his money in another business, he will get a greater return on his capital. He does not think that his decision to sell will have any effect on the company – which is probably true. The problem arises if all the small shareholders think in the same way.

Shareholders who sell for short-term profit are not committed to a company. Their decision making is based solely on short-term financial considerations. British companies do not forego short-term profits in favour of long-term investment because they are constrained by the possible response of the shareholders.

Things are done slightly differently in Japan, where a system called the *keiretsu* applies. Groups of companies and banks hold shares in each other. Company A does not sell its shares in Company B if a low dividend is declared, because Company A knows that Company B would sell its shares in A!

"*As soon as he said 'money isn't everything' I knew we were in trouble.*"

Source: John Morris, *Funny Business*, Business Humour, 1992.

Open Question

Is there evidence of continuing short-termism in the UK?

Companies can make decisions about long-term investment because they know that their shareholders are committed – they will hold on to their shares through short-term low dividends, in the expectation of high dividends in the future.

Trade unions and decision making

Many people have very negative ideas about trade unions. They see them as troublemakers or even as 'the enemy within', trying to control the actions of business and government.

They say that trade unions limit 'management's right to manage'. They make business uncompetitive by fighting any changes which would affect their members. Management does not have a free hand in decision making, because decisions have to be agreed with trade unions, whose objectives are not the same as those of the management.

A manager's view

'The problem is that, when we want to make a decision, our criteria are "What is best for this business?" When we go to the trade union with that decision, they look at it and ask, "What is best for our members?" The two are not always the same.'

The Conservative government elected in 1979 believed that legislation was needed to control trade unions. It introduced a wide range of Acts which have changed the relationship between employers, employees and trade unions.

Trade union legislation: views for and against

'The aim of the legislation has been to crush the power of the trade unions. They can no longer effectively look after their members' interests.'

'The aim of the legislation has been to give management a free hand in decision making. This will make British industry more competitive.'

'The aim of the legislation has been to give management a free hand in decision making. This will result in poorer quality decisions.'

Open Question

Are trade unions a constraint on managers' right to manage?

Some people now say that the legislation has made the trade unions accountable for the havoc which they can cause by irresponsible industrial action. Businesses can be run more efficiently because they can make the necessary decisions and know that they can be implemented without interference from the trade unions.

Other people are asking whether the balance of power has been tipped too far in the direction of management. Are trade unions now too weak to protect the reasonable rights of their members?

One person's view

'It all started with the miners, I suppose. They went on strike about pit closures – to protect their jobs. There was very little sympathy for them and all we saw on the media was picket line violence.

'They were beaten and throughout the 1980s trade union .rights and powers were steadily eroded. No one at the time seemed to think this was a bad idea. Workers did not need to be involved in decision making. They were unqualified and, anyway, they were doing well enough.

'Things have changed recently. People who thought, "I'm all right, I don't need a trade union to safeguard my rights" are now beginning to wonder. Management seems to think that, with high unemployment, it can do what it pleases. No one cared when it just affected poorer people. Who made a fuss when school cleaning was contracted out and the school cleaners were made redundant one day and then re-employed by the new contractors the next day, on worse pay and conditions?

'Well, it's now beginning to happen to the middle classes. Big changes in the civil service, redundancy in the armed forces – look what they have done to the police! People who thought they were "management" are finding themselves put out of work by the real "management". In a funny kind of way, it's justice.

'I think there is going to be a radical change in the way that people perceive trade unions. People who thought that they didn't need a union are now finding that they do. But the union doesn't have the power which it used to have – and they supported the legislation which stripped it of that power.'

2 External constraints

Legal constraints

Some businesses resent certain constraints. They argue that their freedom is unfairly curtailed by legislation. An example of this is the minimum wage rates which were legally imposed on firms by Wages Councils. These have now been abolished but minimum wages could be introduced in the future as they have been in many other countries. And there are many other legal requirements on business.

Some businesses have found that legal constraints force them to look at their practices more carefully and have, in fact, opened their eyes to new possibilities. **Equal opportunities** legislation has enabled women to take a more active role in the workforce, with benefits both to themselves and to the businesses for which they work.

The Equal Pay Act of 1970 (amended by the Equal Pay Amendment Regulations 1983), the Sex Discrimination Act 1975 (amended by the Sex Discrimination Act 1986) and the Race Relations Act 1976 legislate against discrimination and businesses must comply with this legislation.

The Equal Pay Act requires that the contract of an employee must not be less favourable in its terms than that of an employee of the opposite sex. This means that you cannot pay a man £100 a week for doing a job and a woman only £80 a week for doing the same job. Employers have tried to get around this legislation by claiming that women do different jobs from men and giving them different job titles, but the courts have ruled that, if one job is equivalent to another, pay must be equal.

The Sex Discrimination Act makes it unlawful to discriminate against someone on the grounds of his or her sex. Direct discrimination is where someone is refused a job on the grounds of their sex. You cannot refuse a man a job as a secretary just because secretaries are usually women. On the other hand direct discrimination can be lawful if a job needs someone of a particular sex. It would not be unlawful to advertise for a man to play Othello!

Indirect discrimination is more common. This is where a company does not overtly say, 'We will discriminate against such and such a group,' but by its actions actually does so. For example, a company had an agreement whereby part-time workers were made redundant before full-time workers. This was held by the courts to be discriminatory, because most part-time workers were women who had to work part-time because of family commitments.

The Race Relations Act is very closely based on the Sex Discrimination Act and makes it illegal to discriminate unlawfully against someone on the grounds of their race.

Business decision making is constrained by equal opportunities legislation. This legislation aims to give everyone, regardless of race, gender or physical disability, an equal chance of employment. If a business decides to employ only men or only white people, the law will prevent it from doing this. Unless there is a good reason to the contrary, a business cannot refuse to employ disabled people, although it seems that many firms discover such 'good reasons' all too frequently.

The next section will concentrate on equal opportunities legislation as it affects women, but it is very interesting to look at the way in which some businesses have responded with initiatives to tap the skills of black or disabled people. Legislation is a constraint but it can bring benefits to all.

Women in the workforce

Although there are a great many women in the workforce today, there are still jobs which are thought of as 'men's work'. Engineering is one of them. Rapid advances in technology mean that highly skilled engineers are very much in demand by industry. The skills required to be an engineer – analytical thought, numeracy, problem solving – are not confined to men. But it is still the case that the working environment of an engineer may be quite a hostile one for most women.

Positive encouragement and inspiring role models are usually needed before a sector of the labour market in which there has been discrimination becomes genuinely open.

How does equal opportunities legislation *benefit* a business?

Equal opportunities in practice

'In the beginning, I thought of equal opportunities legislation as a bit of a pain. I didn't want our freedom to hire and promote who we liked constrained by the law.

'Now, I'm rather a convert. The legislation made us look at people who we would never have thought of before. I've got two women who job-share in my department. Before, I wouldn't even have tried it. Now I think it's brilliant. I've got two "sets" of skills and experience instead of one. It's a real case of 1+1=3. It's not just women, either. I've got two men who job-share – one is doing a course, so needs two days a week off. The other one's got two kids to bring up on his own. I suppose that, if equal opportunities hadn't made us look at alternative ways of working, we'd never have got the women and would have lost the men! That really would have been bad for the company.'

Equal opportunities is a constraint, but it is a constraint which forces companies to think about their staffing in a fresh way. If that enables them to put in place systems and structures for more flexible working, which means that they can retain skilled and talented staff, then an equal opportunities policy offers the business a benefit.

Benefiting the business

'Before equal opportunities legislation, we were writing off a huge number of talented, willing people, even before we had seen them.

'Now, we have to look at people we wouldn't have looked at before and it's worth our while.

'We're letting ourselves make a proper choice, out of all the people who could do the job. Our prejudices used to constrain us. Equal opportunities legislation has set us free!'

The political and economic environment

One of the most important external factors affecting business decision making is the state of the economy and government policy.

Taxation

Interest and tax rates affect businesses directly. Low interest rates make investment projects cheaper to finance. A period of high interest rates and gloomy business expectations may make many businesses unwilling to invest, reducing demand for firms which produce investment goods. Corporation tax takes a share of profit. VAT requires considerable resources to administer.

Aggregate demand

Income elasticity

The level of aggregate demand will clearly have an impact on sales and therefore profits. High interest rates decrease the amount of money which consumers spend in the high street. A period of tight monetary policy can create difficult trading conditions, particularly if the product concerned has a high income elasticity. In contrast, cheap mortgages and low interest credit mean that people have more to spend.

People often assume that all businesses welcome governments which cut expenditure. This is not necessarily true. If the spending is on capital projects it will be welcomed by many businesses which provide services to the government and depend on government expenditure.

A civil engineer's view

'Of course, what the government does affects us directly. We are civil engineers – building roads and bridges mainly. Very, very little of our work is private. The problem is that, to prosper, we need a government that is committed to spending money on infrastructure. Our decision making is almost entirely constrained by government policy. If they don't spend money, we're stuck! Of course, if we are not doing well, our suppliers suffer. If the government chooses to save money, say by not replacing a stretch of road, we have no work. If we have no work, our suppliers and sub contractors have no work – and so it continues.' – Leslie Staynings, civil engineer

Some people differentiate between government capital expenditure, on such things as construction programmes, and revenue expenditure, such as welfare payments and salaries for public sector workers. They argue that business welcomes and depends on capital expenditure, which is a good thing, but suggest that revenue expenditure ought to be tightly controlled. For this reason, they support tight control of welfare payments.

There are, however, other ways of looking at this.

Effects on small businesses

'We rent out televisions and video recorders. Some people say that these are luxury goods, but if you are unemployed and pretty well stuck at home all day, they are an absolute necessity. You'd go mad without them. A lot of our trade is from unemployed people and it really worries me when they talk about trying to get people off the dole – giving them incentives to take low paid jobs – or cutting their benefits. That would hit our business very badly. We depend on unemployed people. If their benefits are cut, we'll be on the dole too!' – Manager of a TV rental business

His neighbour, a small supermarket owner, made much the same point: 'If you give the unemployed or people on low incomes slightly more money, they will spend it – they've got to. It will be spent locally and will boost the local economy. If you give the richer people more money, they might spend it, but not in my shop. They'll go and buy another luxury car or whatever! That's no good to any of us here.'

Businesses are affected not only by the *amount* the government spends but also *how* it chooses to spend it.

Changing markets

Change management

An organisation has to make decisions about the future and about how it will operate in a market which is rapidly altering and over which it might have little control. For instance, people today are more concerned about the environment and so companies are under pressure to be 'environmentally friendly'. If you go into a supermarket, you will see more 'green' products than ever before. Being 'green' is a selling point for some companies. Look at the way the Body Shop markets itself as a company which is concerned with environment issues, and the way companies take pride in their use of 'recycled' or 'recyclable' materials.

Open Question

Are businesses genuinely concerned about the environment or is this another example of the cynical exploitation of a market opportunity?

Social cost

The 'green' lobby has increasing political power and businesses will have to comply with European anti-pollution regulation. In this way, 'the environment' is a constraint on business activity. But, as with other constraints, there can be benefits. If the extra cost of environmental friendliness can be passed on to the consumer in the form of increased prices, there need be no real constraint.

Many businesses have created benefits by looking carefully at their processes and procedures – by 'mapping' what they do. They then look at this 'map' to see where the greatest environmental damage is happening or where the largest quantity of resources is being expended. Once the most damaging or resource-hungry processes have been identified, they can be targeted for investigation and improvement.

3 Should the major constraint on decision making be financial?

Cost cutting

Since profit is the difference between cost and revenue, any firm wishing to increase its profits can concentrate on either lowering the first, or raising the second, or doing both. In practice it is generally easier and cheaper to cut costs than it is to raise revenue, and cost cutting is very often the first reaction of any firm which is in financial difficulties. But even when a firm is not in trouble it will seize on what it perceives to be 'fat', sometimes without consideration for the long-term effect on customer satisfaction. The following case study illustrates the point.

The inns and outs of cost cutting

Rob Maurice manages a pub. It is owned by a company which has a chain of similar pubs across the south of England.

'I suppose that everything had got rather slack,' Rob admits. 'We were doing all right and profits were good enough, so there was no real need to try to improve things. The owners weren't that interested in what we did – as long as we were making money, that was OK with them.'

Early in 1985, a new company bought the chain of pubs. 'It changed almost overnight. An accountant came in from head office and went through my books. He said that, bearing in mind our turnover, the costs were far too high. The business was being run inefficiently and, if nothing was done, we would be shut down. They were going to send someone in to sort things out.'

The following week, a business manager arrived. 'He wanted to cut costs by 10% straight away. To be fair, it wasn't too bad. It wasn't really a case of cutting back – more of using our resources more efficiently.'

The cleaners' hours were cut back, with very little effect on the appearance of the pub. The pub was quiet from Monday to

Thursday so the bar staff went from two to one on those days. Extra help was employed for Friday, Saturday and Sunday. 'With a 10% reduction in costs, our profits rose and everyone felt more secure.'

Although, financially, the pub looked healthier, Rob was concerned. 'When you looked at the trade in general, people didn't really want "drinking places" any more. They wanted somewhere to go for a drink, but they also wanted food and pleasant surroundings. Look at the number of pubs which are restaurants too, or have family rooms. I felt that we had to make a move. I approached the owners to get permission to turn one of the bars into a restaurant and to build on a conservatory, to use as a family room. I was prepared to put up the majority of the money myself, because I couldn't see us surviving without it.'

Rob was surprised by the response. 'They agreed straight away. I suppose they reckoned that if I was willing to put my money in, it had to be a safe bet. I got a builder in and we sorted out the restaurant area and built a really nice conservatory onto the back, overlooking the kiddies' play area. All through that summer of '86, we were packed out. It was great.'

In the autumn, there was another visit from the owners. 'I couldn't believe it when they said that I had to cut my costs by another 10%. I pointed out that I had pushed revenues up by 20%, but they didn't want to know. Head office had decreed a 10% reduction in costs across the board and that is what I had to do.'

Rob explained that he couldn't cut costs any more. 'I had trimmed off the fat a year ago. OK, so my costs had gone up a bit again, but that was because of the restaurant. People wanted a quality service – people want the place where they eat to be light, warm and well maintained. To be honest, the customers were not that bothered about the cost. They would accept slightly higher prices in order to eat somewhere nice, and bring the kids.'

Rob's argument cut no ice with the owners. A 10% cut was decreed and Rob had to go along with it. Fewer staff were employed in the restaurant and the conservatory, being expensive to heat, was often closed.

'It was a complete disaster. We lost most of the trade we had built up – they went to other places, which were run by landlords and not accountants! I agree that you have to control costs, but there are times when costs are not the only thing you have to consider.'

Management accountants are responsible for gathering information on the costs incurred by a business, along with its revenues, and presenting them to managers to use as a tool for decision making.

In some cases, it has been suggested, the role of accountants is slightly different. H. T. Johnson and Robert Kaplan, in *Relevance Lost: The Rise and Fall of Management Accounting,* Harvard Business School, 1987, are concerned about the way accounting is being used in decision making.

They argue that accounting in business should be a way of helping managers to make decisions. An accountant should provide managers with information on the relative costs of different courses of action and keep them up to date with the financial position of their part of the business. The managers should be able to make decisions on the basis of the information provided by the accountant *and any other information they feel necessary.*

This means that a decision does not have to be made on financial grounds alone. A manager might choose a course of action which is not optimal on financial grounds, but which helps to achieve some other, perhaps wider goal.

Johnson and Kaplan argue that accounting has ceased to be a way of helping managers to make decisions. Instead, it has become the yardstick for determining management success or failure.

The accountant decides whether a manager or a department is a success or a failure on the basis of short-term costs and revenues – what they earn and what they spend in that accounting period. This pushes managers to make decisions on financial grounds alone. Accounting periods are quite short (usually a year) and so managers are forced to sacrifice long-term plans for short-term financial performance.

Tom Peters agrees with this:

> 'Our fixation with financial measures leads us to downplay or ignore less tangible non financial measures, such as product quality, customer satisfaction, order lead time, factory flexibility, the time it takes to launch a new product, and the accumulation of skills by labour over time. Yet these are increasingly the real drivers of corporate success over the middle to long term.' – Tom Peters, *Thriving on Chaos,* Pan Books, 1987

He argues that:

> 'Cost reduction campaigns do not often lead to improved quality: and, except for those that involve large reductions in personnel, they don't usually result in long-term lower costs either. On the other hand, effective quality programmes yield not only improved quality, but lasting cost reductions as well.' – Tom Peters, *Thriving on Chaos*, Pan Books, 1987

Value analysis

The mistake often, and understandably, made by a firm which is in trouble is to cut costs (There Is No Alternative: TINA). But this very action can hasten the firm's demise. It is no good cutting costs if quality is so badly affected that people do not want the product any more.

Value analysis starts from the premise that the consumer must not see any reduction in perceived added value. The product must perform as well as it ever did, it must look as good as it ever did and in every sense remain the same in the purchaser's eyes. Sometimes you can even add value.

Take the ring pull on canned drinks. They no longer exist. Now canned drinks have a section in the top which can simply be depressed. Not only is this cheaper to produce, it saves consumers time and effort when opening the can, and saves the problem of disposal at the same time as being safer.

The critical question to which each component is subjected is, therefore: 'Can this be made more cheaply without any sacrifice in quality?' One way to answer this question is to look at competitors' products to see how they do it. Most manufacturers buy their rivals' goods, take them apart and put a price on each component. They also examine how each one is manufactured and assembled to see if anything can be learned. The Japanese are past masters at taking rival products and then making them better but at a lower cost, and this goes a long way towards explaining their economic success over the past forty years.

Open Question

Is there such a thing as built-in obsolescence or are manufacturers simply responding to consumers' desires to replace those items with which they have become bored?

Another method of answering the critical question is to examine the contribution of each component to the total product. Everyone accepts that goods wear out, and so long as the lifespan is considered reasonable by purchasers, from the producer's point of view, in an ideal world every component would collapse simultaneously. Any component which lasts years beyond the rest is simply over engineered, and therefore costs too much.

4 Quality as a criterion for decision making

What is quality?

'Quality' is something of a buzzword in business today. Look at newspapers and magazines: many companies trying to sell their products and services or recruit staff emphasise their commitment to *quality*.

Most firms have to compete on quality as much as on price or any other feature. A serious difficulty in delivering quality to the customer will be a real constraint on the business. Competitive advantage goes to the company which can combine a keen price with quality and the other characteristics which customers are looking for. But what does quality really mean?

What are the criteria for deciding whether the following products are good quality?

a) A pair of Wellington boots.
b) An army tank.
c) A haircut.

Some people argue that it is impossible to give a definition of quality which could apply to everything, because the criteria are different in every case. However a quality product is one which is designed to meet the requirements of the customer and is produced in accordance with the design specification.

Who is responsible for quality?

Finding out what the customer's requirements are can be difficult, but we have seen how companies such as IBM are working on ways of doing this. Making sure that goods (and services) are delivered to those standards is a further problem. Some business thinkers argue that you have to change the culture of a company and make everyone in the organisation obsessed with quality, from the management downwards.

'Now step back and take a look at your calendar. Are you spending as much time controlling the quality of your department's output as you are investing in cost and schedules? ... If you don't have time for quality and don't value it enough to be interested in it, how can you expect your employees to? ... Plant managers hold production status meetings in which quality, schedules and costs are reviewed. Normally, schedules are addressed first, then costs, then quality – if there is time ... [But] if quality is really the most important factor, then it should be first on every agenda.' – Jim Harrington, IBM, quoted in Tom Peters, *Thriving on Chaos*, Pan Books, 1987

One method of involving workers in decision making is to form a **quality circle**. This is an idea which gained popularity in Japan in the 1960s and 1970s and was introduced into this country by Japanese firms, such as Honda.

A quality circle is a small group of staff, who meet together on a voluntary basis to work out problems. The idea behind quality circles is that it is the staff who have the problems – the *owners* of the problems – who are best placed to solve them.

They have the information and the experience and they know which solutions are likely to work. Also, if it is the staff themselves who suggest solutions to problems, they are far more likely to make those solutions work. As we have seen, it is impossible to expect workers to take part in decision making if they do not have the relevant skills, so training will be necessary. Also, workers need to feel confident that they will be listened to by management and that their ideas will be taken seriously.

Total Quality Management (TQM) is a method designed to ensure high quality by preventing errors from happening.

TQM

'Introducing TQM into our company needed a total change in "mindset". I'm a secretary. I am a supplier – of services, such as administration – to my boss. I am also a customer – of the word processing operators. My boss is my customer, but she is the supplier of services to our customers. Everyone has two roles, which link them up into what we call a "Quality Chain".

'The customer determines the level of service which is required by the supplier and the supplier tries to satisfy the customer. It's a useful way of thinking about your job – you're always asking "What can I do to satisfy my customers better?" It's customer focused.

'The Quality Chain makes you accountable for your own work. If my "service" is not up to scratch, my boss will want to know why. Equally, if the services I receive are poor, I can complain.'

If a company is to produce quality goods or services, it needs some way of making sure that every good or service is of equally high quality. To ensure this, the processes which the business employs will be documented and regular audits will be made, to check that these processes are being adhered to.

Collecting data

'It was only when we actually documented our processes that we could look carefully at them and see where improvements could be made. Writing down what we actually did made it clear that some things were very inefficient indeed.'

Data are collected about the processes which are carried out in the business.

Recording data

'Data recording comes first. The tools are cheap and simple: pencils and chalk. Give those simple tools for recording data to each operator. Then make it a natural part of the operator's job to record disturbances and measurements on charts and blackboards. The person who records data is inclined to analyse and inclined to think of solutions.' – Richard Schonberger, in *World Class Manufacturing*, cited in Tom Peters, *Thriving on Chaos*, Pan Books, 1987

These data are used to monitor the processes and to make sure that everyone is adhering to them.

Once the company has data on its processes and products, it can look at whether it is keeping up with its competitors. First, the company asks its customers, 'What is the difference between an ordinary supplier and an excellent supplier?' and sets its standards on the basis of that information. It then finds out how the best companies meet those standards and applies those techniques to its own processes. This technique is known as *best practice benchmarking*.

BS 5750

BS 5750 sets standards for systems of quality control. It does not itself provide any specific standards for individual products. The procedures for ensuring quality control are set by the business for itself. The business which is registered under BS 5750 is able to show that its systems are effective. It has complied with the criteria set by BS 5750 and that shows that its quality control monitoring systems are reliable.

Many large companies use BS 5750 as a way of deciding between competing suppliers, and many small businesses have been forced to apply for BS 5750 in order to tender for contracts.

Some companies have begun to question the value of BS 5750.

> ### Quality control
>
> In his article in the *Guardian*, 18 April 1993, Stephen Halliday quotes a manager talking about BS 5750 certificates. '... it has nothing to do with the quality of the product going out of the gate. You set down your own specifications and just have to maintain them, however low they may be.'
>
> Halliday argues that BS 5750 certifies that a firm has a quality control process in place; it does not certify that the products themselves are of high quality.

Other people argue that, although BS 5750 can be cynically manipulated by firms providing poor quality products, if it is used in conjunction with benchmarking and total commitment to quality, it is very valuable indeed.

Some conclusions

Business studies is all about organisations and practices which are changing rapidly. For this reason, it is not a static discipline; it is impossible to 'learn about business studies' once and for all. All this book can do is to talk about what is happening in business at the moment, but things change all the time. Just because something is commonly accepted wisdom or an exciting new idea, that does not mean that it is right.

A recurring theme in this Enquiry is the way that constraints turn out to be opportunities. In facing up to the challenge, the business may be able to bring about healthy changes which strengthen its long-term outlook. A cost cutting exercise may turn up all kinds of potential savings which have not hitherto been considered. An environmental constraint, once accepted, may allow the company to present itself as operating in a highly ethical way, thus creating a marketing point in its favour. A serious attempt to overcome a quality constraint may improve customer appeal and end in the company capturing a larger share of the market. A commitment to equal opportunities may end in increasing the range of potential talent available to the company. Even a macroeconomic constraint such as a recession may have a silver lining. The business which is forced to reassess its approach may emerge from a period of slack sales with much increased productivity and therefore lower costs and an improved competitive advantage.

There are times when this book may appear to have given a rather confused message. On the one hand, it suggests that decision making must be systematic; information must be gathered and processed with as much sophistication as possible, and carefully considered criteria must be applied. On the other hand, it promotes the idea that there is a role for an intuitive approach, in which non-quantitative elements are the primary focus for consideration.

Though these ideas may seem to conflict with each other, in reality they are complementary. This is, firstly, because decision making is usually very complex and any rational approach should be included in the range of possible strategies for tackling the problem. Secondly, the strategies which are chosen will vary according to the nature of the decision. The right choice of approach, or combination of approaches, will be different for each decision. This book should enable the reader to approach each decision in an informed and thoughtful way, and devise an approach which recognises the specific features of the decision and the background against which it is to be taken.

The case study on pages 114–17 closes this Enquiry because it embraces a considerable range of the ideas introduced in this book. It illustrates the balance which is needed between quantitative and qualitative arguments. It shows how constraints may make themselves felt on the management team. The reader should now be able to comment critically on the way the problem was tackled.

Wateley Park Hotel

The background

Wateley Park is a 20-room hotel in a south coast seaside resort. It is a private limited company, owned and run by the Wateley family. It is about a mile from the beach, standing in 10 acres of grounds.

A new hotel has opened in the town, in direct competition with Wateley. Apart from being newer, it is better equipped and nearer to the beach. The management team gets together to decide what to do.

They begin by writing the problem on the board:

A new hotel has opened up in the town and is in direct competition with us.

They then brainstorm a whole range of possible responses to the problem.

Similar options are grouped together. Some options fall into more than one grouping. Each grouping is given a name.

The family generated six main options – six possible responses to the new hotel. They then fill out exactly what they mean by each option, so that everyone is clear what they are talking about.

What constraints will the fact that Wateley Park is a private limited company have on the decision-making process and on the decision itself?

The Wateley family have waited until the new hotel has opened before starting to make their decision. What ought they to have done?

What are the advantages of brainstorming as a technique?

This stops the meaning of the options being changed throughout the discussion, with people then talking at cross purposes.

The options

1 Move upmarket
  ■ refurbish hotel
  ■ advertise in Sunday supplements
  ■ refurbish the restaurant

2 Move downmarket
  ■ cut prices – accept lower margins
  ■ cut costs – lower prices
  ■ advertise at BR station

3 Change image to family hotel
  ■ sales promotion – children go free
  ■ family rooms
  ■ sales promotion – senior citizens go cheaper
  ■ week-end breaks

4 Do nothing drastic
- cut costs – maintain prices
- increase spend on advertising

5 Get out
- sell up and retire

6 Offer other services
- open a cafe
- open a camp site
- refurbish the restaurant

The criteria

With the options generated, the family turned to the criteria …

'The first thing we thought of was the cost. In financial terms, we didn't want to waste money, so, all other things being equal, one option was preferable to another if it cost less. This was the "cost" criterion'.

'But cost wasn't the only criterion. We were worried about the amount of management time that would go into whatever we chose. If you spend too much time managing change, important everyday things get neglected. The easier the change was to manage, the better we liked it. We called this criterion "hassle" which described it and expressed our dislike for it!'

'We're a family business and most of our staff have been with us for years. Whatever we do, we want to spare them as much trouble as we can. We had to include "staff misery" as a criterion'.

Remember – these are not the only criteria for decision making. They are only the ones which the family thinks are important.

Why did the family want to call the criterion 'hassle' instead of 'management time'?

Why did the family talk about 'misery' instead of 'motivation'?

These three cost criteria were put into the model. The family decided they were all short-term pains, so used the term 'short-term pain' to sum up all three criteria.

Short-term pain: the cost criteria

1 *Financial* – the hotel management doesn't want to waste money.
2 *Hassle* – the more management time is wasted on the change the less time is devoted to running the hotel.
3 *Staff misery* – this is a family business dependent on the goodwill of staff, who are loyal and hardworking.

The benefit criteria

'The benefits were more complicated. The "image" of the hotel was the first thing we came up with. We have all put years into the business, so the image it has, both to the customers *and* to us, is very important.'

'"Profit" was a difficult one. We didn't know exactly what effect each of the options would have and we certainly didn't have time to spend costing everything out in detail. But we've all been in the business for years and years, so we could say, "Well, this will be a lot more profitable than that".'

'A strong capital base is essential for future development and it has a vital feel-good effect too – we all want something to pass on to the next generation. So we used "capital growth" as a criterion.'

*What does '... the image it has, both to the customers **and** to us' mean? Why is the image of the hotel to the family and to the staff an important criterion for decision making?*

This model for decision making is based on preference scales, so exact figures are not always necessary. What are the advantages and disadvantages of this method of decision making? What safeguards do you need when using this method?

The benefit criteria – image, profit and capital growth – were input into the model and called 'long-term benefit'.

Long-term gain: the benefit criteria

1 *Image* – the hotel's good image has taken a long time to build up. Its loss would be a severe blow.
2 *Profit* – hard to quantify, but at least each option could be put in some sort of order.
3 *Capital growth* – essential for any future development, but also as a 'feel-good' factor. It would feel good to have something to pass on to the next generation.

A quantified approach to the decision making process

The hotel's management team allocate points out of ten for each of the categories of costs and benefits. They are then **weighted** because, for instance, management feel that the financial cost of the short-term pain has, in the end, to be five times as important as staff misery, and so on. The final figures therefore reflect both the initial score and the weights. Taking the family hotel option, the cost is given 7 points multiplied by the weight of ten to give 70; hassle is 6 times 8 (48) and staff misery 3 times 2 (6), giving a combined total of 70+48+6 = 124.

The completed table looks like this:

Criteria and weight	Cost criteria				Benefit criteria			
	Cost	Hassle	Staff misery	Weighted score	Image	Satis-faction	Capital growth	Weighted score
	10	8	2		5	2	1	
Do nothing	5	0	0	50	5	2	1	30
Downmarket	6	4	8	108	2	0	0	10
Family hotel	7	6	3	124	7	9	8	61
Services	8	9	4	160	6	4	5	43
Upmarket	10	10	2	184	10	10	9	79
Get out	0	6	10	68	0	2	10	14

The next job is to make these figures easier to understand, by graphing them. It immediately becomes clear that Option 2 (Downmarket) is definitely out, because both Option 1 (Do nothing) and Option 6 (Get out) give more gain with less pain. Option 4 (Services) is out too, because Option 3 (Family hotel) gives more gain with less pain.

Given the evidence, what should the management do, both in the short and the long term?

Index